RADIO J[

G000277513

A Very English Struggle

by

COLIN KING

To Noel

Enjoy – it's a great read –
it honestly happened!

Kindest

Neil Young

30/12/2019.

Published by the Larks Press in association with
Colin King

Printed by The Lanceni Press,
Fakenham, Norfolk

October 2007

Reprinted by Newprint and Design Ltd,
Fakenham, Norfolk

December 2017

British Library Cataloguing-in-Publication Data
A catalogue record for this book is available
from the British Library

ISBN 978 1 904006 40 4

Foreword

This book is dedicated to the thousands of people who gave of their time to fight for the cause of free radio and in particular Radio Jackie. There are too many of them to name individually but if you stood in the rain on a cold January day, looking out for the Home Office to raid, if you presented programmes or read the news or if you simply stood outside the Radio Jackie offices in Worcester Park in 1985 defying the authorities, then this book honours you and thanks you.

I have always felt that the story of Radio Jackie was so compelling that it had to be told. It has extreme highs and abject lows. It is the story of a group of youngsters who had a dream. Over the years they stayed faithful to that dream as events took them on a rollercoaster ride that saw them openly defying the government and facing the inevitable consequences.

This is not a 'blow-by-blow' documentary because I felt that the overall thrust of the story had to be maintained in order to be readable. Several characters have been merged into one in order to keep the story simple. If you are one of those 'merged' people, I apologise; however what you did was obviously worth recording, so thank you.

This is also not a technical treatise on pirate radio. Nowhere will you find me discussing the relative merits of the 807 transmitting valve compared to the 813. If you are seeking that then I suggest you tuck yourself up with the manual. However if you want the red-blooded swashbuckling story of Radio Jackie then the tale you are about to read is for you – furthermore it really did happen.

I would like to thank Susan Yaxley of the Larks Press for her patience and good humour and for agreeing to publish this book.

The majority of the photographs in this book were taken by Nick Catford. As well as being a consummate broadcaster, he is also a highly talented photographer and I thank him for letting me reproduce them.

I would also like to thank my wife, Angie, who has spent many tortuous days carefully scanning the photographs for publication. This was not an insignificant task and I have really appreciated her support.

I would like to thank my daughter-in-law Melanie, who was the first to read my original manuscript. It was she who told me that the story raced along and that she always wanted to turn the page. She also gave me a brutally frank critique, which was exactly what I needed. I feel her suggestions made this book more readable.

Finally, last but by no means least, my heartfelt thanks to Tony Collis who, at great personal expense, turned our dream into a reality. He is a man with an exciting vision for the future of radio and as long as he is around, the dream of 'Free' radio lives on.

This book is my own personal experience. There was a great deal of hard work but it was great fun. I hope you agree.

Colin King
2007

In memory of

Lucille (Molly) Catford

7th September 1920 - 14th April 2007

and

Jack Maxwell Catford

21st March 1910 - 12th September 2005

also

Brian Malcolm Horne

9th January 1939 - 19th January 2017

CHAPTER ONE

So there we were. Guilty as hell. Standing in a row beside the road with the policeman feeling in his pocket for his notebook.

'Now don't any of you even think of moving,' he hissed as he extracted his pencil and licked the point.

All six of us squirmed. I looked across to Howard. He smiled reassuringly. He had hidden the transmitter in a nearby bush. I had hidden the cassette recorder in the front garden of the house opposite.

The policeman would never think of looking for it. The car battery lay for all to see. He had come upon us so quickly that we hadn't had time to hide that. But he didn't notice the car battery, assuming it had been dumped and therefore was nothing to do with illegal broadcasting: Radio Jackie.

Eric Gotts of the Radio Interference section of the Home Office would most certainly have searched for everything – and found it. But he wasn't here.

'Now let's start with your names and addresses.' He looked straight at me and I began to blurt out my details.

I glanced down the road. Something moved. It was behind the police car.

'Good afternoon officer. Does there seem to be a problem?'

It was Brian Horne. A man at least ten years older than the rest of us, dressed in a crumpled suit and wearing a well rehearsed quizzical, if slightly indignant, look. He always reminded me of a cross between the Artful Dodger and Arthur Daly and today he was in his element.

The policeman didn't respond.

Brian walked up to him, carrying a clipboard that had appeared from nowhere, and with his best worried expression, said, 'Is there something the matter with my boys?'

'Your boys?'

'Yes Officer, my boys; they are with me. Now, what seems to be the problem?'

'I suspect these boys of illegal broadcasting and I am getting their details before we go down to the station to check things out.'

Brian looked dismayed, 'There must be some mistake Officer. You see they're on a sponsored walk that I have organised for the Royal Marsden Hospital.'

The policeman flickered a slight uncertainty and Brian moved in to take command. He turned to us, 'Now boys, I'll sort things out here. I want you to move on to the next checkpoint or they'll be wondering where you've got to. I'll deal with this Officer.'

We nodded and shuffled away, breaking into a purposeful walk until we were out of sight.

Brian, meanwhile, turned to the policeman and in a matter of fact way, using the clipboard to add weight, 'This is a sponsored walk. Can I put you down for a pound?'

And he got it!

Brian Horne

CHAPTER TWO

'*...No man will ever forget Monday August 14th 1967.*' These were the closing words of Johnny Walker's 'Man's Fight For Freedom' promo on Radio Caroline in those few months after the Government had closed down all the other radio pirates.

I had never, until then, realised quite how powerful governments were. One day we had all the pop music a young lad could wish for and the next there was nothing...

Six weeks later Radio One had started bringing us the 'delights' of Jimmy Young singing to his piano. Also Raymondo, 'What's the recipe today Jim?'

In just six weeks we had swung from a diet of uninterrupted 60s pop music to this turgid, state-controlled pap.

The pirates were exciting, fresh and deliciously naughty. They gave us what we wanted and we wanted it to carry on.

The Prime Minister, Harold Wilson, and his left-of-centre Labour government saw these ships as the detested manifestation of free enterprise. So they closed them down.

I was furious in a way I have never been before or since. But I remember vowing to myself that I was going, somehow, to bring back that wonderful mix of music, that had so fired up the youth of this country and spawned the 'Swinging England' of the 1960s.

It was an amazing time. 60s pop, The Beatles and The Rolling Stones were the towering icons.

They say that if you can remember the 60s – you weren't there! But Monday August 14th 1967 stays indelibly etched on my memory. Even now, 40 years later, I still feel the sense of loss, even though the anger has softened to resignation.

I joined the Free Radio Association (FRA), worked on the Committee and hosted the rallies in Trafalgar Square in 1968, 1969 and 1970.

The 1968 rally took place exactly one year after they banned the pirates. Thousands filled Trafalgar Square. . I was hosting the rally which meant that I wasn't where the *real* action was happening.

We had organised for a small group of us, within the FRA, to launch a publicity stunt specifically for the rally - a land-based pirate called Radio Free London. At that time there was only the BBC to listen to, Radio Caroline having been towed away earlier that year on March 3rd.

The Cold War was at its height. The American government was beaming high–powered radio propaganda into the Iron Curtain countries. It was called Radio Free Europe. The choice of the name Radio Free London was therefore deliberate and provocative.

The immediate reaction within Trafalgar Square was one of awe. Quite a few of the crowd had brought transistor radios and as news circulated that we were broadcasting to the rally, small groups formed around their nearest receiver. The atmosphere of bitterness and resentment towards the government was overtaken by the thrill of this obviously illegal station. For the first time in six months, they were free to listen to something that had not been produced by the BBC. It was naughty and it was delicious!

In Fleet Street, the reaction was beyond our wildest dreams. It hit the front pages of every national daily paper and the story ran and ran for several days.

Buoyed up by all the publicity the team decided to carry on until they were closed down by the authorities. In 1968 that authority was the Post Office. Its role included all aspects of communications, including telephones, radio interference, as well as delivering the mail.

It took several days for them to close down the station. Nobody had tried to be a land-based pirate before, so the Post Office was not skilled at tracking illegal broadcasts.

However, there were other factors that conspired to make the job of the Post Office officials harder, one in particular which makes me shudder to this day.

Radio Free London came from a flat in West London that backed onto a railway line with overhead electricity cables, high-power electricity cables.

To put out a decent signal on medium wave, you need to have an aerial that is over 200 feet in length. It must be as high as possible. Must not touch anything. And has to be secured at the far end by an insulator.

Somehow, our guys got this aerial over the top of these lethal electricity cables, carrying several thousand volts, and secured it, via the insulator, to the handrail of a fire escape on the tall building opposite. It was foolhardy in the extreme and could easily have ended in tragedy.

However, the effect of this location was for the railway lines and also the overhead cables to re-transmit the signal, which meant that the authorities could not get a definite fix on where the transmitter was. It was quite literally coming from everywhere.

I suspect that it was a physical sighting of the aerial that eventually led them to it.

Radio Free London carried on and on; finally three days later, Stanley Smith of the Post Office arrived and closed down the station.
I was told many inflammatory stories about the raid. They included likening Stanley Smith to the Gestapo and doors being kicked down in order to access the flat with the transmitter in it.

The reality was less exciting. Stanley Smith and his small team knocked on the door of the flat. They were quite insistent. It was opened.

One of our guys, an engineer, to pass the time and to do the owner of the flat a favour, was repairing his radiogram. The bits sat on the table with the valves glowing.

Smith, upon seeing this said something like, 'I think I shall take this.'

At which point Smith and his team seized the glowing guts of the radiogram and left.

Our guys were a bit shaken, not having been raided before. However, they had the good sense to switch off the transmitter, which actually was in the bedroom and, throughout the raid, was still broadcasting.

The following day, the national dailies splattered their front pages with news of this raid. The twist was that the handrail of the fire escape on the building opposite belonged to the BBC. None of us had a clue about that but – hey – it was good publicity.

Stanley Smith

CHAPTER THREE

The rally in 1970 was a wholly different affair. Much had happened. Harold Wilson was no longer Prime Minister. The pound had been devalued and the political gloom of the 1970s had begun to set in.

However, on that bright sunny day in Trafalgar Square, we were celebrating the victory of Edward Heath and his Conservatives: the party that had promised to bring us commercial radio.

It was a difficult rally to hold together because we were no longer protesting. The huge crowd wanted to hold a march because that was what happened after rallies. But why? And where should we march to?

I remember sitting on the plinth of Nelson's Column, with my microphone, quietly trying to explain why we did not need to march any more. The battle, as I reasoned, had been won. The new government was talking to us and was promising to introduce commercial radio within the near future.

In our minds, we had confused the concept of commercial radio with that delicious diet of non stop pop that we all loved so dearly.

The rally droned on. I introduced a number of the heroes of the pirate ships. Introduced our President, Sir Ian MacTaggart, then said my 'bit' and the rally wound down.

I climbed off the plinth and sat for a few moments, gathering my thoughts from what had been a difficult day.

It was at that moment that one of the 'nutters' that radio seems to attract came up to speak to me.

He was a good 20 years older than me, with short but unwashed hair standing upright, wild eyes peering through NHS glasses, a mouth that had every alternate tooth missing on the top jaw. Grubby nylon shirt inside a cigarette-ash-stained suit and flat feet that plodded in a strangely spaced gait, that I later learned was down to spending many years at sea in the merchant navy.

Enter Maurice Ogden.

CHAPTER FOUR

Maurice Ogden was one of those people who you pray will not sit next to you on the bus. He was wildly eccentric and looked it. Yet he changed my life.

He was barely capable of looking after himself, yet was an amazing man when it came to electronics and transmitters.

He lived in Greenford in a bungalow that was his workshop. He was the director of a film processing laboratory which I later discovered mass-produced blue movies. A guy would arrive with a suitcase from Holland, hand over money and film and rapidly disappear into the night.

Maurice would describe it, with his manic giggle, as *wedding photography*. He would pause and then add, 'well perhaps a little later.'

He had a cat called Caroline. The fact that it was male never seemed to bother him.

The bungalow in Greenford was barely habitable. At some stage there had been a kitchen with all the units. These still existed but the floor, that should have been covered with Marley tiles, was bare concrete.

The consequence of this was that the concrete in the kitchen was smeared with Kit-e-Kat, blood from dead mice and quite probably worse, especially as the cat sometimes would get accidentally locked in.

Maurice's solution to this hygiene problem was, to him, as scientific as it was perfectly logical. He would, first of all, wash the floor. Then he would liberally sprinkle it with Ajax scouring powder. When the floor was white with powder he would flood the floor with bleach and rush out, slamming the door behind him, before the chlorine gas overcame him.

He would return the following morning when the chemical reaction had died down. He was confident that he had the most hygienic kitchen in London. However, in that house, nothing ever passed my lips without it being thoroughly boiled or properly baked first.

He was proud of the fact that he was a doctor of medicine. On one occasion, with a flourish, he proudly produced his certificate. He had bought it in a bar in Liberia. This meant that on his Liberian registered ship he could be the Medical Officer, as well as its Radio Officer.

I am sure that he was quite ready to remove an appendix, with the aid of Grey's Anatomy, a sharp knife and, who knows, maybe even Ajax and bleach!

Fortunately, for all concerned, his skills as a surgeon were never required. Although, judging from his genius in engineering, I would not have liked to have bet against him being successful.

With all seriousness, he explained to me, 'The human body is just like a transmitter - only a bit more sloshy!'

Maurice was the master of invention and *make do and mend*. One night, years before, he was the radio officer on a ship sailing down the St Lawrence Seaway between the U.S.A. and Canada. It was night and it was the middle of winter.

The St Lawrence Seaway is one of the busiest shipping lanes in the world. It was at that moment that Maurice decided to try a little experiment with his transmitter. He was convinced that a different aerial array, together with some modifications to the power transformer of the main ships transmitter, would produce a significant increase in power and therefore range.

Unfortunately for Maurice, his wiring had not been too careful and this, coupled to other endless 'adjustments' that he had made, meant that the whole of the electrics of the ship was in a dangerously poor state.

It didn't just blow the fuse, it quite literally blew the fuse-box off the wall. The ship was powerless. No steering, no lights, no radio, NOTHING. It just drifted, invisible and uncontrollable in one of shipping's major motorways.

The Captain, or 'The Old Man' as Maurice called him, was rather concerned. Perhaps that was an understatement. The problem was what to do. There was other shipping but also there was pack-ice and icebergs.

Maurice had soon come up with the solution. He grabbed a large chunk of wood and with a sledge hammer drove two rows of six-inch nails into it.

He connected up the generator to one row of these nails and then began the task of restoring power.

First of all he connected up the steering to a nail, then smashed it with his sledge hammer into one connected to the generator. There was a mild explosion. The sledge hammer flew out of his hand in a shower of sparks as the nails welded themselves together. But the ship could steer itself again.

Next came the lights, another explosion, another shower of sparks, sledge hammer flying across the room, more welded nails, Maurice grinning in manic way and suddenly the ship was visible again.

Slowly the whole ship came back to life: under control and back on course.

No doubt the Captain couldn't decide whether to be grateful for rescuing the situation so effectively or throttling him for getting them into that situation in the first place.

I know how he felt...

CHAPTER FIVE

'Well I do know this transmitter engineer called Maurice Ogden,' I heard myself saying.

That's brilliant', my brother, Robin, replied. 'Almost everything is in place. Do you think he would build us a transmitter?'

'Yes, I'm sure he would ... but I have one of the old Radio Free London transmitters, it's an old German medium wave field transmitter. I haven't a clue how to run it properly but maybe Maurice could do it.'

We both paused and took a deep satisfying pull on our pints and smiled conspiratorially. It was all coming together.

There aren't many places in Britain where you can sit outside in your shirtsleeves on 1st November at 11 o' clock at night. In 1970 that is precisely what my brother and I were doing.

The place was the enchanting harbour at Hugh Town in the Isles of Scilly. We had sat on the harbour wall for a couple of hours: talking radio and occasionally refreshing our glasses from the nearby Mermaid pub. Now it was well past closing time, yet we were loath to move. We were excited by what we had decided. It was all going to be so simple ... or so we thought!

Maurice would run the transmitter. We would use techniques unheard of in 1970s land-based pirate radio (and avoided to a great extent by the BBC). It was 'compression' and 'limiting' and this made the station sound louder and more exciting. It also made the signal more effective.

Without going into too much technical detail, compression is where you take a quiet sound and make it louder. Limiting is where you take a loud sound and make it quieter. The effect is to make the sound you are transmitting have a constant and predictable volume. Once you can rely on this constant volume then it is a simple matter of making sure that the transmitter plays this at the maximum volume before it starts to distort the sound.

The effect is a startling increase in the loudness of the station.

We would pre-record programmes and get several presenters that we knew to record one hour each.

Both Robin and I enjoyed radio with a bit of pace and purpose. Since the offshore pirates had been banned, radio in Britain had stepped back considerably. However, much as we wanted the return of the pirates, we felt that even their mix of music was too slow for what we envisaged.

We concluded that the way that radio would have to go would be towards non-stop music. So we decided to make the station's sound be just that: NON-STOP MUSIC – no dead air. One great record to run into the next and the DJ was to just hang on in there, interjecting where he could.

14

It was how we were going to be totally different from Radio One and from what the new commercial stations would have to sound like, once they started.

From my contacts with the government, via the Free Radio Association, I knew that there was going to be a legal restriction on the number of records played per hour. In other words, non-stop music was not just going to be discouraged, it would be ILLEGAL.

We were determined to show, by example, what fast-paced music radio should sound like, in the hope that this would be copied and force the government to relent.

Robin then looked at me and said, '...but what are we going to call this station?'

We sat looking at each other, our glasses almost empty and we started the process of deciding upon a name.

I recalled a meeting I had had nearly a year before with four 'spotty' teenagers, Nick Catford, Dave Owen, Howard Smith and Mike Hayes, in Sutton, Surrey, who boasted that they were going to start a land-based pirate local radio station to serve south west London and North Surrey.

'...but what are you going to call your station?' I had asked.

One of them looked at me and said, 'We are going to name our station after the daughter of President Kennedy.' My heart sank.

'So you are going to call the station Radio Caroline then?' I replied.

The apocryphal story of how the founder of Radio Caroline, Ronan O'Rahilly, had decided upon the name came from a picture that he had seen on a copy of *Time* magazine whilst on a flight back from the U.S.

The picture showed Kennedy and several leading members of his administration, on the floor of the Oval Office playing with his three year old daughter, Caroline.

At that moment Ronan O'Rahilly decided that if Caroline could bring the administration of the world's most powerful country to their knees, then that was going to be the name of his radio station.

I looked back at these four young men, 'That would be fine whilst Radio Caroline is off the air ... but what if it came back? Then you would have an identity problem.'

Their faces flickered; they had accepted my point. My mind was racing. Could I think of another name quickly? JFK ... John Fitzgerald Kennedy. Radio John ... yuk! Radio Fitzgerald ... double yuk!

Then I said, 'How about naming your station after the wife of President Kennedy?' I paused, 'Radio Jackie?'

They looked at me, giving nothing away.

'Radio Jackie' I repeated, 'No, it doesn't have that nice ring to it like Radio Caroline.'

At that point I dismissed the name outright.

Six weeks later, they were on the air using the name Radio Jackie. So I can claim to have been the first person to have put the words 'Radio' and 'Jackie' together. However, I cannot claim to have named the station.

I then turned to the obvious leader of this group, Nick Catford, and said, 'You're going to get caught.'

He looked back at me defiantly, 'Yes I know, but we don't care. If you believe in something this passionately then you have to keep going. We will succeed and the government will give in and give us a licence.'

Nick Catford being interviewed by Thames Television

'Brave words!' I said to my friend, Robin Rose, who was with me at the time, as we walked away after the meeting. 'I don't give those kids six weeks before they give up.'

Well over a year had elapsed and those young lads had been persistent. Transmissions were confined to Sundays and they were frequently raided ... but they were still on the air.

Back on the harbour in the Isles of Scilly, I looked back at my brother. We both wanted a name that represented what we wanted to achieve. We had both laughed, several weeks before, listening to some unknown pirate blowing twice on the microphone and announcing that he was 'Radio Egg and Chips' and then playing a highly distorted record.

This was so much what we wanted to avoid.

Robin then said, 'We could use Radio Kaleidoscope.'

Mentally I tried to spell it.

'There was a small group in Essex who used the name but they've disbanded. There is also a theme tune, "Kaleidoscope" by the group Kaleidoscope.'

He continued, 'I could make some jingles in my studio in Holland and ship them over to you.'

I still struggled with the spelling but the more I thought about it, the more I like the imagery of it. Kaleidoscope – forever changing, brightly coloured and strangely pleasing. Yes that was it.

So Radio Kaleidoscope was born.

CHAPTER SIX

The warm balmy breeze of that November night in the Isles of Scilly abruptly changed to wet and cold once I had returned home to Brockham in Surrey.

Maurice was excited with the prospect of launching the station and readily agreed to operate our transmitter.

FIEND HORT MIT – is the legend that was on the front of this German field transmitter. It was designed to be mobile on the battlefield. It was the size of a narrow bedside cabinet but required a trained weightlifter to move it. Mobile? Forget it! Some German with a strange sense of humour had fitted a handle to the top. It was a sick joke. It was more likely to dislocate your shoulder.

Then I learned that that was not all. It needed a power pack.

'What's a power pack, Maurice?' I heard myself asking. I thought it just needed to be plugged into the mains.

'Well Colin, it needs some grote ironmongery.' 'Grote' was Maurice's word for huge and very heavy.

The plan was to launch Radio Kaleidoscope on Boxing Day. It was a good day because the guys working for the Post Office Radio Interference Department would be at home with their families celebrating Christmas. Therefore we could broadcast without the fear of getting raided.
'Can you get a power pack ready for Boxing Day?'

'I'll need to get a large transformer but that shouldn't be a problem.' I gave him the money to buy this chunk of ironmongery, confident that with the balance of November and the best part of December still to come everything would be ready for our initial broadcast.

WRONG.

Maurice bought the transformer and began work but despite this the power pack remained in bits for several weeks!

He had decided to investigate the transmitter more thoroughly so that by Boxing Day, all we had was a floor covered with assorted parts.

I patiently shrugged and suggested that perhaps it might work better if it was re-assembled. Maurice laughed, lit yet another cigarette and wedged it in the gap between his teeth and began soldering. The smoke floated up behind his glasses causing him to blink profusely.

Kaleidoscope was not going to happen this Boxing Day.

By New Year's Day the transmitter was back together again and Maurice had begun work on the power pack.

The transformer was about one foot square and made of solid metal: an iron core with copper windings around it. Lifting it put you in danger of getting a hernia.

Quite how the Germans expected this transmitter to be portable, I don't know. It would have been better if they had built it into a small truck. At least, that way it would have been on wheels.

In January 1971, the Post Office were on strike for several weeks and this we assumed included the Radio Interference Department.

So the launch date was set for the last week of this strike.

Maurice was keen for the broadcast to go out from his bungalow in Greenford. The previous Sunday, Maurice and I had rigged up an aerial in his garden but the power pack was still in bits.

On the Wednesday, my phone jangled with an excited Maurice.

'Colin, it works! The blighter only works.'
'Well done Maurice, does that mean you've put the power pack together?'

'Well ...' pause, 'it is a bit of a lash-up.'

I soon learnt that 'lash-up' was slightly better than 'NO' but not a lot.

When I arrived on the day of the launch broadcast, the power pack was still in bits. However, wires had been soldered connecting the various parts. It quite literally covered the dining room floor.

'It does look a bit of a 'lash-up' Colin, but it works.'

I looked at it and made a mental note never to go anywhere near it.

CHAPTER SEVEN

So the day of the first broadcast had arrived. The transmitter sat on the floor in Maurice's dining room. The 'lash-up' power pack spread out ominously in front of it.

My brother Robin had flown in from Holland to be there.

We decided to launch Radio Kaleidoscope at 11 o'clock, and Maurice duly switched on the transmitter. I remember looking nervously at 'the lash-up', but Maurice was true to his word, it worked.

Cigarette wedged between one of the gaps in his teeth, wild-eyed and happy, Maurice tuned up the transmitter and right on 11 a.m. we were on the air.

We had four hours of pre-recorded programmes to transmit and based on the result of that we would see how we could take the station forward.

The first hour was 'wild'. It was made by The Geeter: The Geeter with the Heater, the Big Boss with the Hot Soss.

I still have a recording of that first hour and it is unlike any radio programme I have heard before or since. It was 'wild'. Absolutely NO dead air, 21 records played in the hour and the use of a device called a 'Copycat' that produced some very exciting sound effects.
The second hour was made by a delightful guy called Terry Davies. Terry was one of the stalwarts of the ship-based pirate Radio Northsea International (R.N.I.). Again there was no dead air: non-stop music. Terry Davies is one of the most polished and professional presenters I have ever had the pleasure to meet. To get him on our programming team was a real coup.

My brother recorded the third hour under the name of Phil Hazelton. He later became known as 'Uncle' Phil Hazelton and specialised in playing Golden Oldies.

Robin and I had persuaded a friend of ours, Mike Baker to make the final hour. Mike Baker and Noel Edmonds had learnt their broadcasting craft together and had both been short-listed for Radio Luxembourg. Noel Edmonds got the job – and the rest, as they say, is history.

Mike Baker was a superb talent and a great acquisition to the programming team.

I read the news.

Maurice smoked prodigiously. Robin had brought him some cigarettes off the plane. Maurice swore that these were much better for him than English ones, because they didn't carry a 'health warning'; they were healthy cigarettes!

He also made and drank endless cups of tea.

Bee Bumble and the Stingers, Nut Rocker, with The Geeter in full flow, this felt great.

I tuned in my little transistor radio and felt for the first time the feeling of elation that broadcasting brings.

We were on 266 meters or 1133 khz in new money. Radio One was down on 247 meters playing their 30% records, chat and 'live' music. How could anyone resist this 'new kid on the block'?

It was about half an hour into the broadcast that a car pulled up outside the house. To this day, I have no idea who it was. They stayed outside for several minutes and then drove off. It could have been a neighbour or some guy picking up his girl friend. More likely it was one of those mysterious people who, upon hearing a pirate station on the air, set out to track it down. Nothing more than that. We grew to accept them as part of what we were doing. Later we gave them a name – 'Anoraks'.

The thought that troubled me was, 'What if it was the Post Office? What if they were to get out of the car and knock on the door? What would we do?'

Maurice suggested connecting the door knocker to the mains electricity. Robin smiled resignedly, looked skywards and dismissed that idea.

'Maurice, what if it wasn't the Post Office, - what if it was people collecting for Christian Aid Week?' Robin's argument was undeniable.

Maurice paused, then brightened, 'It could be the Jehovah's Witnesses?'

'No Maurice, No No No!' I realised though at that moment just how vulnerable we were.

After the car pulled away, there were no more scares from that department.

The Geeter was in full swing, 'All Right Now' by The Free. 'Please God, he was not going to say THAT word!' He did.

It was about then that I noticed a slightly metallic, slightly electrical burning smell. I didn't think much of it at first. 'Quite probably some dust on the unused transmitter,' I convinced myself.

Terry Davies was in full flow. Norman Greenbaum, Spirit in the Sky. Pounding, driving music, yes Radio Kaleidoscope sounded totally different to anything else on the air.

It was then that I noticed that the base notes in that record sounded a bit more distorted than they were supposed to.

Was it our new compressor/limiter, the electronic recording trick that makes the programme sound louder and more powerful? Or was I just imagining it?

The next record started and that sounded distorted too. I mentioned it to Maurice.
'Yes, I noticed it a few minutes ago,' he said and reached for his AVO meter. This is the box that electronics engineers use to tell them what the electricity is actually doing inside the transmitter – or anything else electrical.

He wedged another cigarette between his teeth and started to probe the transmitter. He looked a bit like a doctor with a stethoscope; gently checking here and then checking there.

The distortion was not going away.

He turned his attention to the 'lash-up' on the floor around him: his power pack.

Long, long minutes passed.

'There does seem to be something not quite right with the mains transformer.' He concluded at last. 'Still. It's not that bad, we must carry on.'

Robin and I looked at each other. The distortion was not too bad, so we agreed with Maurice and carried on.

I have since heard it called 'The Frog in the Saucepan'. The saucepan is over the heat and the frog is swimming in the water. The frog is saying to itself, 'Well it's all right at the moment.' It gradually convinces itself that it is safe to stay in the water which is getting hotter and hotter. Common sense would have told the frog to do something and to get out of the saucepan (as frogs do!)

Just like the frog we carried on. Maurice was so persuasive. 'Keep going. The show must go on.'

By the end of Terry Davies' show the distortion was getting so that it was difficult to hear the programme.

'Switch off, Maurice, this is awful.'

'No, I can fix it.'

'Switch it off and fix it.'

'No, the show must go on.' He was adamant.

Robin motioned to me to come with him into the front garden.
'Look at that,' he pointed to the next door neighbour's television in their front room. The picture was throbbing in time with our music.

'That's it, we must switch off.'

When we returned, Robin's Phil Hazelton Show was beginning, though I doubt if anybody could have discerned it from amongst the distortion. Maurice had decided that drastic action was called for.

It was then that I noticed the layers of smoke. There was a thin but distinct layer of white smoke across the room at about three feet off the ground. Above it were clouds of Maurice's cigarette smoke. The situation looked serious.

With great solemnity, Maurice produced a broom, followed by a foolscap envelope.

'If I am going to fix this, I need to know how hot the main transformer in the power pack' (the lash-up) 'is getting.'

'Good, then switch off and you can find out.'

'NO, we can't stop now. I have to place my fingers onto the top of the transformer to see if it is getting hot. Then I'll know what is wrong.'

'Maurice No!' I insisted, looking nervously at all the terminals on the top which, no doubt, carried many thousands of volts of electricity. 'No Maurice, this is crazy.'

Maurice looked me straight in the eye and handed me the envelope, 'This is my Will – you know, my Last Will and Testament. If it bites me, switch off at the mains and lever me off the power pack with this broom handle. You do know how to do mouth-to-mouth resuscitation don't you?"

The thought of doing mouth to mouth on that cigarette-stained mouth and the gap teeth was not one I relished but before I could stop him, he leant forward over the transformer and gently – oh so gently – lowered two fingers between the terminals and felt the heat.

Then he removed his fingers and looked at me with obvious pleasure. 'Yep! I can fix this although it will be a bit of a lash-up.'

A lash-up? Another bit adding to this chaos wasn't going to make any difference now.

Maurice moved with purpose. I remember making a cup of tea for us all as Maurice attached some more bits and pieces to the power pack. Maurice's word for attaching was 'dog' or 'dogging'. 'I just need to dog this onto here,' indicating some part of the lash-up.

Then he removed his cigarette packet. He took all the contents out, laid them on the floor and began tearing the box into strips: cardboard and silver foil. He then started stuffing them into various places in and around the main transformer. I stood by the mains plug and held the broom stick.

Suddenly there was a small electrical crackle and the distortion vanished. We were back on the air with a clear signal.

I realised at that moment how Maurice's Captain had felt after the St Lawrence Freeway incident. He had quite probably got us into it but he had also got us out of it. I was elated.

I peered at next door's TV and it was back to … Normal!

Phil Hazelton gave way to Mike Baker and at three o'clock after no further incidents, we closed down. We had run out of programmes.

We switched everything off and checked that it was all safe.

Then we piled into my car and went round to the Chinese Restaurant. We were starving.

CHAPTER EIGHT

It was an important meal at the Chinese Restaurant. The three of us sat there and, as well as unwinding, we discussed what we had learned.

We were delighted with the programming. There had not been a single second of 'dead air' throughout the whole four hours.

'I felt we were very vulnerable.' I kicked off the topic of security. 'If the Post Office had found us, we would not have had a clue what to do. We were simply unprepared.'
Both Maurice and Robin agreed although Maurice suggested electrifying the door knocker for the second time that day.

'No Maurice!'

He was beaming all over his face and puffing on his cigarette.

'How does Radio Jackie keep going?' Robin asked. 'They do put out a regular Sunday service – and – what's more they've been doing it for well over a year now. So it can be done.'

I explained what I knew of Radio Jackie. They had started by broadcasting from friends' houses. Or to be more specific, from their parents' houses. This approach had failed because as each house got raided by the Post Office, the parents refused to let them do it again.

In the end they simply ran out of houses.

However, what they did have was people. Radio Jackie had a large group of friends and followers who were, to varying degrees, prepared to 'run the gauntlet'.

They had decided that they had to broadcast outside in the open.

I recounted the story of their first attempts when, because the equipment was so heavy, they had put everything into a large pram and tucked it up with a blanket.

The first week had passed without incident. The second week there had been a raid. They had seen the Post Office draw up in their car trying to see where the signal was coming from. They saw the aerial and charged over in that direction.

Nick Catford, Howard Smith, Mike Hayes and Dave Owen, meanwhile had disconnected the 'pram' and pushed it away in the direction of some young families playing in the park.

In their eagerness to catch Radio Jackie, the guys from the Post Office charged past the pram. Nick, Mike and Dave had never looked so innocent in their lives!

After that it was a question of finding a suitable location, rigging an aerial and turning up on Sunday morning. The circle of friends kept watch and when they saw the Post Office official arrive, they blew whistles and everyone scattered.

The very early days of Radio Jackie. Mike Hayes (left) and Dave Owen with the legendary pram

The pram continued to be used for several months. It was wheeled onto trains, into the Underground and was even refused admission onto a bus! Several occasions required catching a tube train from Morden into London and then going out to Hounslow or other suitable areas where an aerial had being erected during the week.

Why public transport? The answer was simple, they were young teenagers and nobody had a car.

Then about six months after they had started they were approached by an older man. At first they thought he was from the Post Office Detection team but he soon reassured them. His name was Brian

Horne and he drove a van. Nick told me, years later, that this was the turning point for Radio Jackie.

Suddenly transportation was no longer going to be a problem. Brian's van could (and did) take them anywhere.

I looked back at Robin and Maurice, 'The main problem was that they were getting quite a lot of equipment confiscated – because it was so heavy.'

'We need to make a smaller, lighter and more portable transmitter.' Maurice concluded.

'The problem is that we don't have that wide circle of friends to call upon.' I added, 'What's the point of having lighter kit if we don't have the time to escape in the first place?'

'We are rather sitting ducks.' Robin agreed.

'We were lucky today because the Post Office was on strike. If the strike is over next week, we won't last two hours.'

'There must be another way,' I heard myself saying.

'Well...' Maurice brightened, 'We could always use meteorological balloons.'

Robin and I looked at him. Maurice grabbed a paper napkin and began drawing on it.
'What is it that tells the Post Office where we are?'

'The signal?'

'Yes, but what else? It's the aerial. They're looking for a 200 foot length of wire and it leads straight to where the transmitter is. Piece of cake. You will get caught every time.'

'What does the balloon do?'

'Two things. Firstly it gives us the near perfect aerial because a vertical 200 foot wire is the best you can get.' He paused. 'But secondly, if we also attach a length of strong fishing line to the balloon and anchor that to a point, say, half a mile away...' His eyes lit.

'Then when they raid, we simply rip the aerial from the transmitter and it shoots off into the sky and can be brought down by somebody who is well away from the action.'

The idea struck a chord with Robin and me. It would possibly buy us time to escape.

Maurice's mind then went into overdrive.

'If I could make a transmitter small enough, we could actually hang it from a balloon or several balloons. It doesn't have to be powerful because it will have height. The higher, the better. Then all we have to do is tether it at two points and when they raid we simply cut the tether that is upwind. It will rapidly fly away, giving us time to retrieve it and escape.'

'But how do we get the programmes up to the transmitter?' Robin asked.

'Simple, we shoot it up a little UHF link that is based at a totally different location but pointing to the balloon. The Post Office will never track it because the signal will be so directional that they would need a helicopter to even get the signal.'

This idea seemed to be worth exploring. At that point, we decided that Radio Kaleidoscope was not going to broadcast again until we had got this idea properly sorted.

We all agreed that we had to stay one step ahead of the Post Office.

CHAPTER NINE

The following week, I bought a supply of meteorological balloons. I also rang British Oxygen (BOC) and got a price for balloon gas. It was a lot of money because I had to rent the cylinder and valve as well. So I hesitated and rang Maurice.

'You don't need balloon gas,' He chortled down the phone. 'We simply make our own hydrogen. Much better lift.'

I thought about the Hindenburg but relaxed when I realised that I wouldn't be travelling in it.

'You know how to make hydrogen?'

'Piece of cake, old man, piece of cake.'

The next few weeks passed and we seemed to make little progress. Maurice was intent on miniaturizing the transmitter. I would visit him every Sunday and every time he seemed to have made no progress. It was always a 'lash-up' but at least each week it was a different 'lash-up'.

Finally my patience gave out.

'Maurice, don't you think we ought to try out the balloon? I mean, we don't know how much lift we can get from it.'

'Good idea, old man, I'll get the materials together and we can do an experiment on Sunday.'

Maurice was true to his word and everything was bought, though not assembled.

'All you do is fill this large glass container with caustic soda and drop aluminium foil into it. The reaction will give off hydrogen which will flow up this pipe and into the balloon.'

It seemed so simple.

Watching Maurice squeezing aluminium foil into the glass container, whilst puffing on the cigarette wedged between his teeth, made me nervous. I had done some physics at school but, for the life of me, I could not remember whether it was hydrogen or oxygen that re-lit a glowing spill with a 'pop'. With the amount of hydrogen that we were going to be needing, I didn't want to be around when he re-proved that hydrogen re-lit a cigarette with a 'pop'.

Images of cartoon faces blackened by exploding cigarettes flashed across my mind. However, Maurice seemed confident that he knew what he was doing, so I relaxed and the experiment continued.

I first became suspicious when the part-inflated balloon lay limply on the ground. With all the lifting power of hydrogen, surely it would have been soaring into the air by now?

'Is that right?' I asked Maurice.

'Not sure, let's have a look.'

'For God's sake, Maurice, take that cigarette out of your mouth.'

'Oh, alright.'

We peered at the balloon. It was filling with something and part of it wanted to sail into the sky. The other part was a mass of water that was lying in the bottom of the balloon.

'That's easily fixed.' Maurice held the balloon with the neck downwards and poured the water out onto the ground. There was obviously something inside the balloon that was lighter than air but it didn't seem to want to get off the ground.

We persisted and soon the balloon was becoming fully inflated. The water was removed but still the lift was nothing like I had expected. I decided to apply the acid test. I tied the 200 foot of aerial to it and gently let the balloon fly away.

Most of the wire lay on the ground. The balloon itself had soared to a heady 30 foot, just clearing a neighbour's house.

Any idea that this was going to lift our miniature transmitter to 1000 feet had gone out of the window. It couldn't even lift the aerial. Besides, I couldn't see us making hydrogen in this way prior to every broadcast.

'I think that the balloon is full of hydrogen *and* water vapour. That's what is stopping it from flying,' concluded Maurice.
The next day I bought a cylinder of balloon gas. The smallest cylinder that BOC sold was five feet in length and needed two people to carry it.

It lay in Maurice's front room for a year before we handed it back and reclaimed the deposit.

The balloon idea was totally impractical.

CHAPTER TEN

'Drones, old man, drones.'

'What the hell is a drone?' I looked at Maurice.
'Drones, that's the future. They're remote controlled aircraft.'

I thought of the guys on Epson Downs with their model airplanes on a Sunday morning and wondered what he meant.

'Drones are huge. They can be up to eight to ten feet wingspan and can carry quite heavy loads. I've got it all worked out.'

I made Maurice a cup of tea and we sat down as he outlined his new idea. He had a large piece of paper and he began drawing on it.

'We know that if we have height then we don't need to have a lot of transmitter power.'

I nodded.

"Well if a drone was doing a tight circle over London at say 2,000 feet then we would put out a fantastic signal and it would cover the whole of the Greater London Area and beyond.'

I was a little cautious about the idea but it seemed worth exploring.

'Go on.' I said, 'But how would we control it?'

'Well, we don't.'

'WHAT!'

'We get other radio stations to do that.'
My mind fogged.

'Look, old man, if I put three little radio receivers into the plane and then get it to fly to the point where the three different radio stations, that they are receiving, are of a pre-set strength. Then I can get it to automatically circle at that point for three hours.'

'But how do we get the drone back?'

'Simple, I reset the three radios and it flies to a new rendezvous point which can be anywhere we choose. One time it could be in Kent, the next time could be in Berkshire or Essex or anywhere we like – so long as the fuel doesn't run out.'

'..And we could bring it down to the ground using the remote control.' I was getting into the idea.
'Then when one drone finishes its three-hour stint, we simply replace it with another. Three or four drones are all we need.'

Yes, technology, that was the way forward. The invention of the transistor had made all this possible. We sat and excitedly discussed the detail of this plan.

'Are you sure you know how to make all this happen, Maurice?'

'Yes, it shouldn't be too difficult. But I will need to build it into the fuselage of the drones.'

My task was to find somebody who not only made drones but was sympathetic to what we were trying to do. Where could I start?

In reality it was not difficult. I checked with the known contacts of the Free Radio Association and rapidly I located a guy in the Sidcup area of Kent, his name was Paul Dunbar.

I had a meeting with him and we agreed to try the idea out. The problem was going to be the building of the transmitter, and everything else, into the fuselage. It was going to have to be purpose-built. For that he insisted that we paid for the drone.

I talked it through with Maurice and my brother and we agreed to stump up the cash between us. However, it was going to be expensive to run the operation that we were planning. We needed help.
Again, the Free Radio Association came to my assistance. The President was Sir Ian MacTaggart, who was a right winger, keen on free enterprise and civil liberties and above all free radio.

I met him at his Park Lane address and after a couple of scotches and a visit to the Playboy Club down the road, we agreed that he would back the venture to the tune of £10,000. It was a lot of money but we were suddenly looking serious. This had to work.

I bought a drone from Paul and after a couple of weeks delivered the fuselage to Maurice's home in Greenford.

32

He worked like a man possessed.

I visited him almost every day but mainly my duties were to keep the great man fed and watered (and supplied with cigarettes). I swear that if I had not done this he would have died of starvation, such was the intensity of his work.

Little electric motors, car batteries, reels of wire and bits, bags and bags of bits filled his home for the next few weeks: transistors and all those electronic components that make guys like Maurice excited and, quite frankly, bore the hide off everyone else.

He did a fantastic job. Not only did it all fit inside the drone but the weight was evenly distributed as well. So the chances of the drone flying were excellent.

I rang Sir Ian and gave him a progress report and he expressed a desire to attend the inaugural flight. In fact he insisted.

We carefully transported the fuselage back to Sidcup where it was reunited with its wings.

'Bit heavy?' I said.

Paul looked at it and said, 'Shouldn't be a problem, these can easily carry this weight.'

We agreed the date of the inaugural flight. It was only going to fly over the South East London and Kent area but this would prove whether it could be done.
I rang Robin in Holland and he produced a special programme for the flight. Of course, it started with Frank Sinatra, 'Come Fly With Me' followed by 'Up Up and Away'.

So the day of the inaugural flight arrived.

We met in a large field just outside Sidcup. When Maurice and I arrived, our man with the drone was putting the finishing touches to the wings and checking the controls. Flaps – yes, rudder – yes, it was a bit like the flight deck of an aircraft. I realised that, although in miniature, all the same checks had to be made. Plus, of course, the remote controls.

Maurice had charged up the car battery that was going to drive the whole operation and we loaded that into the drone. All were present – except Sir Ian.

We waited. Half an hour passed before he turned up. He emerged from his car with almost youthful excitement. He was wrapped up against the September weather as we all briefed him on what was going to happen.

He made a short speech of encouragement. We were so elated. This was our dream come true.

Fuel was loaded onto the drone. A few more checks and the engine was started. A stutter followed by a high pitched roar.

Maurice beamed and puffed on his cigarette.

I stared transfixed by the events. This could be the turning point of my life. I had the idea. I had the equipment and now I had the money as well. Everything had come together.

The drone started to move forward. We watched, holding our breath. It bumped along the field, getting faster and faster. Then – YES – it was airborne. It gained height and flew over the tops of the trees at the far end of the field. Out of sight. Out of control.

Our drone expert was frantically waggling the remote control until his shoulders slumped and he placed it on the ground.

None of us ever saw that drone again. Where it went is a mystery. I just hope and pray that it didn't cause any damage when it eventually came down.

Sir Ian rang me the following day and asked for the balance of his money to be returned.

CHAPTER ELEVEN

Maurice was in a cloud of smoke. One cigarette after another mitigated only by the cups of tea that I was passing to him.

'Where do we go now?' He looked at me as though I was going to come down from the mountain with two tablets of stone.

'I suppose we are going to have to copy the way that Radio Jackie do it.'
'Who do we know that would support us and create a security cordon round the transmitting site?'

'I don't know Maurice, I'm going to have to get on the phone and speak to as many people as I can. Then we see what comes of it.'

Maurice looked like a child lost. He had worked so hard on the drone that now it was all over he had nothing to do.

I added, 'Well, if we are going to run Kaleidoscope the way that Jackie is run, then we are going to need small, light and easily portable transmitters. Something you can simply pick up and run away with.'

Maurice brightened.

'Funny thing that, old man, I was going down Tottenham Court Road in London, this week and I picked up a couple of these...' He produced two metallic components measuring about two inches square and about four inches long. 'If I'm reading these OK then these could solve the problem of the very heavy modulation transformer.'

Imagine trying to lift and run with a block of iron measuring 10" x 10" x 10". It was heavy! It was also the big stumbling block to miniaturising a transmitter.
'When will you know if it works?'

'Well I could make a lash-up this afternoon.' Maurice lit another cigarette and plugged in his soldering iron. He was happy again.

Within a couple of hours, his lash-up was ready. He pulled a wire that ran past his head and out of the window. It was his aerial. He connected it to the collection of 'bits' in front of him and switched on.

I had been worried for some time about his exposure to radio waves. I didn't know that much about transmitters but I did know that the most powerful radiation came from the point nearest the transmitter. I was also concerned about the fact that the lash-up was not screened.

I pointed this out to him. He laughed, 'If it was going to scramble my brains, then it would have done it years ago.'

Even so, I persuaded him to move the aerial further away from his head and shoulders.

I reached for the radio. Yes, there was a clear signal.

'Let's broadcast something,' he suggested with gleeful anticipation.

I produced a cassette of Cat Stevens, Lady D'Abbanville. We both knew that the bass notes on that would test any transmitter to the limit. I switched on the cassette recorder and we listened carefully and critically.

It was fine. Maurice was right. The weight problem had been solved. We switched off the transmitter in triumph.

'Now all you have to do, Maurice, is to put all this into a box with a handle on the top and we'll be ready.'

Maurice nodded.

We jumped into my car and drove down to the local Wimpey Bar. Burger and chips followed by a Brown Derby, washed down with Coca-Cola.

We lived the high life in radio!

CHAPTER TWELVE

'Hello, is that Dave Cliff?'

I held the phone in my hand wondering what this call might bring. I had learnt that in the previous couple of weeks, there had been a 'split' in Radio Jackie and there might now be a group of guys available who knew how to run a proper land-based pirate radio station. This looked like the perfect answer to our problem.

I explained who I was and what we had been trying to achieve. I explained about our programming objectives and how we wanted to show, by example, what real 'music radio' was like.

His voice showed an increased level of interest. I explained that we had Maurice as our transmitter engineer and that we had been able to make kit that was disposable and highly portable.

We agreed to meet and so, on the following day, Maurice and I found ourselves in South Wimbledon driving up a highly respectable road lined with beautiful Victorian terraced houses.

Maurice had put on his best suit. It was grey, ash grey, like his other suit. It might have had an immaculate pin stripe had it ever gone to the cleaners. As with most of Maurice's clothing it was the colour of cigarette ash.

I rang the doorbell. Dave ushered us into the front room where a small group of youngsters sat and lay in varying poses.

We did our introductions. I detailed what it was we were doing and what we hoped to achieve. Maurice showed them the transmitter, which they examined with great interest, concluding that it was still a bit big and still a bit heavy. 'But never mind!' was the consensus.

I played them bits of our programmes to illustrate what we wanted to sound like. I noticed a young lad sitting with rapt attention. He wore glasses and had long blond hair and was about five years younger than me. He listened. We played other examples. He questioned. He listened again.

Dave Owen

Seldom have I ever met anyone who had such a keen ear for music, such an instinctive 'feel' for what sounded right and what did not. Here, I could see was a raw natural talent. It then began to dawn on me that, in 1970s Britain, there were so few opportunities in radio that Maurice and I represented, quite probably, his best chance of getting on air.

His name was Dave Owen.

We talked. Dave Cliff's mother brought in tea and custard crème biscuits and we talked some more.

It was obvious that Maurice and I had exactly what they were looking for and they had exactly what we were looking for. Agreement to join forces was simple.

We agreed to the name of Radio Kaleidoscope. They were from Radio Jackie and had split away. Understandably they wanted little more to do with the station but Maurice urged them to feel more sympathetically towards it.

'Radio Jackie has been broadcasting now for more than four years. It is the flagship station for the cause of free local radio. We can't afford to let it die.'

Maurice looked around at the group and to my surprise they nodded in agreement.

He continued, 'If it ever comes to a matter of Radio Jackie dying, we must rejoin it under the name of Radio Jackie.'

The Crew
Left to right: Roger Allen, Johnny C., unknown, Howard Smith, Pat Edison, Martin Comley, Dave Owen, Dave Cliff,
The car is Jim Crow's Peugeot

He then added, 'Jackie is a cause. Kaleidoscope is a sound. If it comes to it, we can put our sound on Radio Jackie and nobody loses anything.'

It was quite a profound thought from Maurice. He had summed it up very neatly. It certainly impressed the team in that front room.

The mood switched to practicality. It was no longer if they would join with us, it was could we get a broadcast out next Sunday?

I suddenly realised that although these were youngsters, all in their late teens, when it came to land-based pirate radio, they were a bunch of hardened professionals. They knew exactly what they were doing.
As if from nowhere, paper, pencils and maps were produced.

'What frequency are we going to be broadcasting on?' '266 meters 1133 khz.'

They scribbled away and calculated the optimum length of the aerial.

'It will have to be longer than Radio Jackie's aerials.' They looked at each other, shrugged and dismissed the problem with, 'We'll just need trees a bit further apart.'

'How powerful is the transmitter?'

They pored over the map and calculated just how far the signal could reasonably be expected to go.

Then it came to the programmes. We agreed that Dave Owen would have the first hour. Terry Davies would do the second. My brother, Robin, would do the third and a quiet little chap sitting in the corner, Pat Edison, would do the final hour. They explained that Pat had a studio in his bedroom.

I thought, 'Ah! He could be useful.'

I asked if they needed any money and slipped them a few notes. They seemed very content. There were records to buy and aerial wire needed.

Finally Dave Cliff turned to us and said, 'Leave it to us. We will have everything ready for Sunday. We will meet at Dave Owen's house, in Abbotts Road, Sutton, at 8 o'clock next Sunday morning.'

Maurice turned to me, once we were back in the car, 'Wow, old man, I think we've cracked it. I shall have everything ready.'

We had progressed to a new phase of our life.

CHAPTER THIRTEEN

Sunday arrived. I collected Maurice.

It all felt so new and exciting. There we were outside Dave Owen's house and Dave was still in his pyjamas, obviously hungover from the night before. His mother shoved a bowl of corn-flakes into his hand. He spooned some into his mouth and some down the front of his dressing gown. He looked dreadful.

Then, in a matter of seconds, he was changed and raring to go. The transformation was miraculous.

Off we went.

The site was in the countryside. Fields all around but bushes were there providing cover and there were several tall trees. A wire was slung between two of them and dangled down to the ground.

We connected up the transmitter and Maurice fiddled with some knobs. There was a meter on the side of the box with the needle well over to the right. Maurice chuckled with approval.

We looked at our watches. Ten o'clock precisely, we fired off the first cassette with Dave Owen's Show on it.

Dave had created a new opening jingle.

'BROADCASTING FROM LONDON, TO LONDON – ON 266 METERS, THIS IS RADIO KALEIDOSCOPE.'

It sounded great. My respect for this young man increased. He wasn't just an 'also ran'. This guy had real talent.

We were all gathered around the transmitter but soon Dave Cliff directed us off to our lookout positions.

Pat Edison stripping an aerial wire, no doubt removing the fillings from his teeth in the process

I had a car so it was my responsibility to drive around and look for the Post Office. Howard Smith, a delightful guy, tall, thin, angular with the mandatory long hair, joined me in the car and we cruised around enjoying the 'thumping' signal. The programme sounded great. The compression made it sound so loud and powerful.

Maurice's transmitter was working brilliantly.

The way that they were protecting Maurice and the two other guys with the transmitter was by a security cordon.

In order to reach the transmitting site, the Post Office would have to cross an open field. They had placed four guys, each with a loud whistle, on the outside edge of the field. Consequently, if the Post Office raided, all they had to do was blow their whistles which would give the guys on the actual site enough time to get away.

There were two cars that provided protection from the road. Howard explained, 'They will have to arrive by car. I know who they are, what they look like and their registration numbers. If we see them, all you have to do is sound your horn until the signal goes off the air.'

He continued, 'The Post Office have two teams in this area, one led by Jim Crow and the other by Eric Gotts.'

'You know them?' I was surprised.

A typical transmitting site (Note: The two largest items are the car batteries)

'Yes, Jim Crow usually works with Dick Plumb. They're OK. Jim is a great guy. He does his job but I think he understands what we're trying to achieve.' This was all news to me.

'When Stanley Smith retired, Eric Gotts tried to assume control but Jim Crow was given the job. So Jim is in charge of the whole operation. Eric Gotts reports to him and Eric hates that!'

I chuckled, 'So there's office politics in this?'

Lookout

Howard continued, 'You must watch out for Eric Gotts, he's an absolute bastard. To him, closing down pirates is his whole mission in life. If it was left to him he would have us all prosecuted, locked up and the key thrown away.'

Paul Lock on lookout duty

'God save us from zealots.' I replied. I don't think Howard knew what a zealot was but I'm sure he grasped the sentiment.

The Terry Davies Show came to an end and the Phil Hazelton Show began.

'Good.' I thought, 'Perhaps the Post Office will leave us alone on this first broadcast.'

Phil Hazelton was playing a lot of Golden Oldies from the sixties.

Everlasting Love by the Love Affair, drifted into Young Girl, Gary Puckett and the Union Gap. The sound was spectacularly good. The new compression tricks, that we had brought to the sound processing, made us sound immensely powerful. It thumped out of our loudspeaker.

Keith West, Excerpt from a Teenage Opera soon became Scott Mackenzie, If you go to

A highly alert lookout!

42

San Francisco be sure to wear some flowers in your hair.

The sun was shining, the music was good, all was well with the world.

Howard leant across me as I was driving and pressed the horn. He kept his hand on the horn as I came to a halt.

Within seconds, the station was off the air.

'That's Eric Gotts. He pointed to a tall, clean shaven, brown haired man who was climbing over a fence by the field leading to the transmitting site. There were two other men with him, Brian Williams and Vic Frisby. Gotts looked up and then the three of them sprinted across the field and out of sight into the bushes.

Silence.

Howard said, 'Drive around.'

Obediently, I did as I was told. 'Where is everybody?'

'They will have hidden the equipment and then scattered in all directions. Our job now is to pick them up.'

I felt a thrill coupled with anxiety. Is this what it is going to be like every week? I had always been a very law-abiding person so this was alien to me. Then I thought how different the programmes we had put out were to anything else that people could hear.

I recalled trying to rationalise what I was trying to achieve and came to the conclusion that Radio Kaleidoscope was the perfect protest. It broke the one law that I wanted to change and nobody gets hurt.

Its existence was its justification and its justification was its existence.

The British people deserved better radio than the diet that was being forced upon them and we were showing the way.

But in spite of all this rationalisation, I was still pumping a lot of adrenaline! How could Howard stay so calm?

'There they are.' Howard pointed to a small group beside the road. Maurice was in the middle, beaming from ear to ear and puffing hard on his cigarette. He wasn't alone. Most of them were having a smoke. Dave Cliff's car pulled up behind and between us they all climbed in.

43

They were so matter of fact. Then I realised that the job was not yet completed. We had to wait for Eric Gotts and his team to depart and then go back in and see what of the equipment had not been discovered and confiscated.

Half an hour later, in the distance, we saw Eric Gotts and his team drive away.

'OK let's go!'

We pulled up at the nearest point to the site and walked over. At first I thought there was nothing left. Then out of the bushes we retrieved the cassette recorder and the tapes. Followed by two car batteries and the rotary inverter.

'Where's the transmitter?' I asked. I had thoughts of Maurice building a new one from scratch. It had taken months to build this one.

Eric Gotts (right) and team

Dave Owen nonchalantly said, 'Oh, I hid it near that tree over there. When I saw they were coming from that side, I ran across this field on the other side. Bloody hell Maurice, that transmitter is heavy, it nearly killed me!'

The transmitter was where Dave said it would be and so we gathered everything together and drove away.

Broadcasting was over for the day.

44

CHAPTER FOURTEEN

'IT'S A BOMB!'

I looked up startled, the IRA had only exploded a bomb in London a week or so before. There was a middle-aged man standing in the doorway holding the cash till but making no attempt to get away.

'Oh don't mind him, that's Brian Horne.'
The Manager of the Wimpy Bar gave a slightly amused, slightly exasperated look and gestured to Brian to give him back his till.

Brian handed back the till and ordered a cup of coffee. He came over and joined us.

'That was one hell of a signal you were putting out today, boys.' He sat down.

'You heard it then?' I said.

'Heard it? You couldn't miss it!' He exaggerated. 'Jim Crow reckons you were putting out at least a kilowatt.'

Maurice piped up, 'With the valves we were using, we were putting out barely 30 watts, nowhere near 1,000 watts.'

'Did you say Jim Crow?' I was startled because I remembered Howard telling me that he was the head of the Post Office Radio Interference Team.

'Jim said you were so loud that you had to be on high power.'

The guys looked at myself and Maurice and we explained about the techniques we were using to make the sound appear louder and stronger.

Brian listened, '...but it sounded so loud.'

'I know.' I said, 'In the States they use these tricks all the time. The BBC are so hung up on quality that they dismiss what we did today as distortion. But did you think that sounded distorted?'

Brian agreed that it didn't. 'Are you doing this again next week?'

'Yes,' I replied, 'we are meeting on Tuesday, at the Wheatsheaf to sort out the details.'

The conversation babbled on for at least another hour and then gradually everyone began to drift away.

Maurice turned to me in the car, 'What did you think, old man?'

'Great, but what did we learn?'

'I must make the transmitter small and lighter. I think I know how to do it.'

I dropped him off at his house and drove home.

That night I hardly slept. All the events of the day, and in particular the raid, were buzzing around my head.

CHAPTER FIFTEEN

The following Sunday, we broadcast from Morden Hall Park. We were beside a long stretch of water with pylons nearby. I remembered Radio Free London and the effect of the railway lines and overhead cables and thought that would confuse Eric Gotts for a while.

It certainly seemed to because we managed to broadcast almost the entire programme that we had planned for the day.

I was standing by the transmitter with a couple of other guys and we were getting ready to pack up and leave.

Suddenly I realised I was on my own. I hadn't heard the warning. The cassette recorder and other bits had gone but the car batteries and the transmitter were still there.

I looked around to see where the danger was coming from. There was nobody in sight, at first glance. And then I noticed, in the distance, two policemen walking alongside the water towards me.

I pushed the batteries into the undergrowth and grabbed the transmitter. Dave Owen was right, it was very heavy. I lumbered away from the policemen, clambered over a wall, out of the park, onto the road and away.

I was wearing a light brown suit, so I walked down the road carrying it as though it was a briefcase.

Eventually I found a suitable hedge in a front garden of a house and slid the transmitter behind the retaining wall and out of sight.

I made my way back to the entrance of Morden Hall Park. The entire team was gathered together in a group, chatting.
'Did they get anyone?'

'No, what happened to the transmitter?'

'That's hidden.' They all looked relieved.

'I suggest we should split up now because we look suspicious standing here as a group. If the police are looking for us then we're the obvious choice.'

They laughed and carried on talking.

'Well,' I said, 'I really think we should split up. Let's all go in different ways back to the Wimpy Bar. I'll buy the coffees.'

The group did not split but gradually moved in the general direction. I did what I suggested and strolled off ahead. I was no more than twenty paces away from the group when a police car screeched to a halt.

I kept looking ahead, pretending not to notice anything. However, I could hear the group being rounded up.

I reached the end of the parade of shops and turned the corner. I was safe. I turned and peered back round towards the action. They were all standing looking extremely guilty as the two policemen fired questions at them.

Several minutes passed and then the policemen selected three of the group and ordered them into the car. Sheepishly, they did as they were told. The rear doors slammed but the policemen did not drive away immediately.

The Jackie Crew

At that moment I spied a middle-aged man in a suit, striding towards them. It was Brian Horne,

'Officer,' Brian barked. 'What are you doing with my boys?' He had reached them by now and was looking the policeman who was standing beside the car full in the eyes.

'We suspect these boys of illegal broadcasting and we are going to take these three down to the station for questioning.'

'Surely you know, Officer, that broadcasting is a civil offence and not a criminal one?'
'No.'

Brian was in full flow. Once a policemen has shown the slightest doubt Brian would always assume command.

With an air of authority that only Brian could assume, he announced, 'Well broadcasting contravenes the Wireless Telegraphy Act and that is purely a civil offence. Therefore you have no authority to detain these boys.'

He strode across to the rear door and barked, 'Come on you three, get out. These policemen are exceeding their authority and have no right to detain you. Come on hurry up, out you get.'

The three emerged cautiously from the car.

Brian turned back to the policeman. 'Now I will let this go this time, but if you do this again I shall have to take note of your number and lodge a formal complaint.'

I couldn't believe what I was hearing.

The policeman seemed hesitant so Brian opened the front door of the car and motioned him in. 'Now off you two go, but don't let this happen again.' Suitably chastened, the officers of the law pulled away.

The Wimpy Bar resounded to our happy voices, that afternoon. We had put out a fantastic signal, the programmes had sounded great and Brian had rescued the day.

CHAPTER SIXTEEN

Once in a while, land-based piracy throws up larger than life characters like Brian Horne. He was almost a generation older than the rest of us and that carried with it an authority that Brian was always happy to use.

I always maintain that Brian was a highly intelligent man, let down by the education system. As a result, he had learnt to live on his wits. Always exaggerating, always encouraging, always willing to take authority head-on, even if it meant resorting to the most outrageous lies. Somehow Brian always got away with it.

Brian Horne

Quite a few of our team were unemployed. (This was the 70s.) Brian good-naturedly chided them by calling them 'dummies'. He would describe them as 'thick and unemployed' so therefore they were 'dummies'.

One evening with five of us in my car, I asked Brian what he would call one of these dummies if he got himself a job. Brian paused for a moment and then said, 'He would still be thick and stupid, so he's a 'wally'. We laughed. We thought it was a great word: 'wally'. We started to use the word amongst ourselves.

It is interesting to note that the slang term 'wally' for somebody who is 'thick and stupid' passed into common usage in South West London first. I reckon that it was Brian who invented the term in my car.

He is a strange mercurial character who never really sought to lead the group but who gave up his time and energies with a passion and, bless him, was almost always there when we needed him most.

Howard Smith and Brian Horne

It is also one of the strange aspects of land-based piracy that you attract people who just want to watch.

You arrive at your site and switch on the equipment. Within an hour, there will be a few individuals standing on the other side of the field, clutching their portable radios, and just watching.

If you walk over to them, they will often just melt away into the woods. The occasions when you do engage them in conversation, you realise that they are just radio enthusiasts with a rather lonely pre-occupation. We called them 'anoraks'. This was the first time that I ever heard this expression and I often wonder whether we were the people who originated it. Wallies and anoraks, we did our bit to enrich the language!

One Sunday in winter, we were transmitting from a field beside a wood. On the far side of the field stood the motley collection of anoraks. They were doing us no harm, so as usual, we ignored them.

The broadcast was going well. The first three hours had gone out and we were well into Phil Hazelton's show when we suddenly noticed a policeman stride along the edge of the field.

We didn't even have time to hide the equipment; he was upon us. In fact we didn't even have time to turn the transmitter off. Phil Hazelton continued to play his Golden Oldies Show.

How's the signal getting out?

'Now what's going on here?' The officer enquired.

Dave Owen made to reply but suddenly there was a shout.

'OI - YOU - GET OFF MY FIELD!'

The policeman spun around. It was Brian Horne, wearing a crumpled sports jacket with leather patches and swinging a stick.

'What are you doing on my land?' He gestured to the policeman with his stick.

'Is this your field?'

'Yes it is, now get off!'

The policeman was confused, 'I just wanted to establish what was going on here.'

Brian's face became quite irritated. 'These lads are from Kingston College – they are conducting meteorological experiments, with my permission.'

The policeman seemed satisfied.

Brian again turned to the officer. 'Now I would appreciate it if you didn't trample all over my field. I only sowed it last month and this is a

51

crucial germination time. Your feet will do a lot of damage. I want you to leave through the wood.'

The policeman carefully picked his way along the grassy edge of the field and then set off into the wood.

Several minutes later we saw him walking along the road back to his car.

We never went off the air and we finished the entire broadcast that day.

CHAPTER SEVENTEEN

After just a few weeks, we needed to make some organisational changes.

Terry Davies spent most of his time on Radio Northsea International and was finding making programmes for us difficult. So we agreed to let him go. Terry seemed relieved as well.

We needed to ensure a continuity of sound, already we were starting to become 'Five Programmes with a Common Name'. So Mike Baker became Programme Controller. He introduced a predictive Top 40 where he made educated guesses as to which of the new releases would become hits and which wouldn't. Frequently he would place a pre-release record into the top spot at Number One.

Mike had an uncanny ear for a hit record and often his choices were proved correct.

Instances of this ability were; the instant promotion to the top spot of The Hughes Corporation and 'Rock the Boat', also Kodachrome by Paul Simon and of course 'Billy Don't be a Hero'.

Mike Baker worked for Capital Radio as a sound engineer. Thirty years later, under the Freedom of Information Act, we learned that he had been informing the authorities of our every move.

There were times when we were all very frightened by the authorities. The group bravado kept us together and moving forward. However, I can understand how Mike, who desperately wanted to pursue a career in radio, could have been pressured into informing on us.

That said, he did an amazingly good job for us. He broadcast under the name of Denny Tewson and later was the first voice to be heard on Beacon Radio in Wolverhampton.

Another organisational change involved Pat Edison. Pat made the very generous offer of letting us use the studio in his bedroom to record our programmes. His mother and father were delightful people and very understanding. They enthusiastically welcomed us into their home.

If I were to describe Pat, I would suggest he would be an ideal choice as Mole, in a stage version of *Wind in the Willows*. He stood not very tall,

Pat Edison

very quiet but with a whimsical little smile, if ever you managed to glimpse it, because it was concealed behind a mass of long straight hair that hung over his face to his shoulders. To speak, he would often reach up with both hands and part the hair as though it were curtains.

Pat was one of those people who only comes alive in a studio. When Terry Davies left, we put Pat in the 11 o'clock to midday spot, immediately after Dave Owen.

I had some misgivings because all I could see was this quiet little man. Yet when his programmes went out, they were some of the most original and inventive shows I had ever heard. He was a huge talent.

To illustrate this, he approached Mike Baker and myself one day with an idea for a science fiction spoof. He was going to call it 'Captain Zapp'.

I don't mind admitting that I was hesitant. However, I believe that the best thing to do with an idea is to explore it. If it fails you can drop it but if it's successful then that's worth the effort.

The following Sunday Captain Zapp hit the airwaves. It was utterly brilliant. It was an original, tightly edited send-up of the science fiction genre. He couldn't resist the radio related 'dig' on occasions.

Screams and voices expressing horror, 'AAaaaaaagh what's that, it's horrible.' Followed by the authentic voice, edited in saying, 'Hello everybody this is Tony Blackburn here.'

We fell about laughing. It was amazing that this little 'Mole' could produce work of that quality and genius.

Six weeks after the start of Captain Zapp, Kenny Everett on Capital Radio launched an identical science fiction spoof called Captain Kremin and the Krells. It was hugely popular, made a great deal of money for Kenny Everett and was a straight copy of Pat Edison's work.

We were outraged at this blatant copy but I reflected that this was what Radio Kaleidoscope was all about. We were openly trying to set the pace for broadcasting standards and here was evidence that Capital Radio in London was listening to us and taking notes.

They say that imitation is the highest form of flattery.
Another organisational change was the introduction of a mailing address and a telephone number for the station.

Maggie Stephenson

This came about in the form of one of the most stunningly beautiful women I have ever had the pleasure to see: Maggie Stephenson.

Maggie was an ambitious woman, well spoken and did a wonderful job answering the telephone when we were broadcasting. It gave us a contact with our listeners.

Her husband was Tony Rocket, a great character and a distinctive broadcaster. He projected on air exactly the way he was when he was away from the microphone:

charming with a gentle sense of fun. We were lucky enough to persuade him to fill the 2 p.m. to 3 p.m. spot.

So Kaleidoscope was set up. We could contact our listeners, run competitions and receive mail.

The on-air line up was:

Dave Owen	10 a.m. to 11a.m.
Pat Edison	11 a.m. to midday
Denny Tewson	Midday to 1 p.m.
Phil Hazelton	1 p.m. to 2 p.m.
Tony Rocket	2 p.m. to 3 p.m.

It was a settled line-up and worked well.

CHAPTER EIGHTEEN

As time went on, Maurice began to produce smaller and lighter transmitters. I would go round to his house and there he would be sitting beside a transmitter. Frequently it would be on and without any screening and the aerial running past his head and shoulders.

Again and again I urged him to use things called 'dummy loads' and also to take more care. But Maurice was never the sort of person to take care. He was in his element.

He lost that appearance of being someone you did not want to sit next to on a bus. He had a 'bridge' inserted in his mouth, which did wonders for his appearance. The only down side was he broke numerous cigarettes trying to stuff them into the gaps in his teeth that were no longer there.

Despite his improved appearance however, he was still far from perfect; still looked very wild, smoked like a chimney and his suit, still uncleaned, was an even paler version of cigarette ash grey!

He still had that anarchistic sense of humour.

Several Sundays, we broadcast from his mother's house in Coulsdon which was unoccupied as she was in a care home. We were never raided at this location and to this day I do not know why we didn't use it more. Maurice was more than content for us to use it but we always felt we had to keep moving on.

The other amazing thing was that Maurice was never raided at his own home in Greenford. Perhaps it was because he was putting out intermittent signals as he tried and tested differing ideas.

Maurice was always fascinated by the transmitter that Radio Northsea International used. It was called an Ampliphase transmitter. He did not have a clue how it worked and this bothered him.

I told him all I knew about Ampliphase transmitters, which was precious little. 'Maurice, you take a signal, split it 180 degrees out of phase, amplify both sides and put them together.' That was the extent of my knowledge.

The following week Maurice had built an Ampliphase transmitter. He had taken the theory and buoyed by the fact that it could be done, went ahead and constructed it.

I had told him it could be done and he then had the knowledge and intelligence to do it. I call that genius.

Maurice was also intrigued by a system called Delta Matching. This is a technique where a transmitter is not connected to the base of the aerial but at a point further up. He reckoned that we could Delta Match a transmitter to the line of lamp posts in the middle of the A4, Western Way. His belief was that by using strong magnets to make the connection to the lamp posts, we could put out a powerful signal on Long Wave to rival Radio Two.

The Post Office had been working on his telephone system back at his film laboratory. I suspect that this was where he obtained some Post Office barriers and lights because he produced these rather like a magician pulling a rabbit from a hat.

I was extremely sceptical but I was persuaded so at 2 o'clock in the morning, we conducted the experiment. Maurice's theory meant the strong magnets needed to be connected to the lamp-post in two places. It worked, but quite how well we never knew because we failed to tell anybody to listen and report back!

Even at 2 o'clock in the morning there were plenty of cars and I was heartily relieved when Maurice eventually decided to end the experiment.

The idea would never have worked anyway because we could not have broadcast from the middle of one of London's main arteries at midday on a Sunday. The traffic would have been roaring past, doing its steady 50 m.p.h. in a 40 m.p.h. zone. Even in the mid 1970s, it was a crazy idea.

I was dedicated to the cause but not suicidal.

That summer we had a long hot spell, which dries out the soil. This was not good news for us because we relied on moisture in the ground to make the signal effective. We used to hammer copper tubes into the ground and connect them to the transmitter. These were called earth rods and on the whole these were very effective, but not in dry weather.
One Sunday morning, during this hot spell, we tuned up the transmitter and the signal was very poor. The meter on the side had a needle that should be pointing over to the right. Today it was barely half way.

Dave Owen's show was going out. It was a shame that the signal was so poor. Maurice, forever resourceful undid his flies and began to urinate on the earth rods.

'What the hell are you doing, Maurice?'

'Salt water, old man, salt water. Pee on the earth rods. The more you pee the higher the signal goes.'
We laughed. This was two-fold. It was an eccentric way of making the signal better.

At the time, the BBC was embroiled in a Payola scandal where they were accused of taking money to promote records. He was, of course, referring to 'The More You Pay – The Higher the Record Goes.'

'The More You Pee – The Higher The Signal Goes,' struck a chord with us all.

Dutifully we all peed on the earth rods. It was a hot day and for some it was a struggle. Maurice even resorted to whistling encouragement. We drank a lot and the signal was a lot better by the end of the day.

Shortly after this, one Sunday morning, Maurice pulled me to one side. 'I say, old man, I'm a bit worried. I can't feel the left side of my face.' To illustrate this he pinched it hard.

The following day I drove him to see his doctor. The doctor referred him straight away to a specialist.

Within a week, it was diagnosed as a brain tumour. The transmitters had fried his brain after all.

The following Wednesday he had the operation and he was quite bright afterwards. The feeling had returned to his face and he was very positive.

Six weeks later Maurice died.

CHAPTER NINETEEN

Tony Collis emerged from a hedge by the road near Leatherhead Golf Club. He had been caddying, had a few pence in his pocket and was happy.

He was a tall, slim lad with long ginger hair that somehow never looked right on him. His manner and maturity belied his fourteen years of age.

Tony Collis

Brian Horne was sitting beside me in the car, 'There he is, over there. That's Tony.'
I stopped and he climbed in.

Almost immediately he and Brian began an argument. It was good-natured but Brian was flying one of his flights of fancy and this fourteen year old was having none of it. Tony stood his ground and after a few moments they agreed to differ and the conversation drifted onto other things.

We drove back to Tony's house where I met his parents. I shook hands with his mother who was a quietly determined lady. His father was a lean, fit man of medium build who had an air of being an 'out-doors' man. The couple were fiercely independent, illustrated by the fact that they had built the house they were living in. I soon realised that this independence had rubbed off onto Tony.

Brian pulled me to one side, pointed to Tony's father and whispered, 'He works for the Post Office.'

I had visions of his being one of Jim Crow's men but as it transpired he was on the telecommunications side of the Post Office. Today it is better known as BT.

Tony led us up to his bedroom. There was none of the expected posters or record players. This was his workshop: a table that was his workbench in the corner, and soldering irons and neatly stored racks of components. I noticed three fruit machines standing along one wall.

He saw my gaze. 'Oh, they came out of a pub. I'm trying to get them working again.' I didn't think any more about them.

Upon that table sat an aluminium box measuring barely more than a foot square. It had a handle on the top.

It was a transmitter and when I lifted it, it weighed just a few pounds.

'Did you make this?' I asked. Tony looked indignant. He didn't need to answer, the look said it all.

I was impressed.

Tony switched on the transmitter and I was relieved to see that he had a genuine respect for the equipment; none of these unshielded transmitters that had proved so fatal for Maurice.

Brian and I climbed back into the car and drove around assessing the signal. It was perfect. None of the spurious signals that Maurice's transmitters frequently used to emit.

This was clean. If Tony could maintain this standard then there was no way that anybody could accuse us of interference with 'aircraft and shipping'.

I had a long chat with the lad. I liked him. I liked him a lot. He was unlike any of the others on Kaleidoscope.

I looked again around his bedroom and noticed once more the fruit machines. I smiled. 'Boys and their toys!' I thought. I could not have been further from the truth. These were faulty fruit machines that Tony was repairing. Then he was placing them into pubs and being paid a rental income for them. For a young guy he was extremely enterprising.

We chatted long into the night and I explained my dream about music radio and how I really wanted a licence that would enable us to show the rest of the radio industry how exciting music radio could be. We discussed our attitudes towards Kaleidoscope. We agreed that we were not pirates but simply unlicenced broadcasters.

We considered what we should do when we did get the licence. We agreed that we simply wanted a shop front on the high street, where anybody passing could drop in and be welcome. The studio should be to the front of the building so that passers-by could see the 'action'.

We both agreed that outside the studio, in the street, we would have a large model pirate. This was to constantly remind everyone where we came from and what our roots are.

Eventually he agreed to take over from Maurice.

The following Sunday we used his transmitters for the first time. Tony stayed with the transmitter throughout the broadcast, constantly checking the signal. We came to expect this level of conscientiousness from him.
Tony insisted upon using his own equipment. This left the obvious question of what to do with the transmitters that Maurice had made.

It was about that time that rumours started to emerge of the dreaded Eric Gotts pushing to get Jim Crow removed from his job. We knew that Jim Crow, who was a delightful man, was not showing his bosses much confiscated equipment.

Jim would be content for us to turn off the transmitter. He had closed down the station. As it transpired, that was the fullest extent of Jim's authority. Eric Gotts, on the other hand, was consumed with a hatred for illegal stations and established the practise of grabbing equipment and proudly parading it in front of his (and Jim Crow's) bosses.

Eric Gotts' star was in the ascendant. Somehow we had to keep Jim Crow in the top job.

Tony looked at me with a sly smile and suggested, 'Can't we "feed" Jim with bits of Maurice's equipment? That ought to stop Eric.' This young lad was 'street-wise' and old beyond his years!

Gradually, over the following weeks and months we left all of our old equipment on Jim Crow's doorstep. On Monday morning, as he left for work, he would collect the 'present' on his doorstep and take it into the office. Whether it kept Eric Gotts at bay we will never know but he never got the top job, so perhaps Tony's strategy worked.

We established an excellent rapport with Jim Crow. He knew that we were not going to stop, so he operated accordingly. More importantly he operated within the law.

It was not unknown for him to ring us up on a Friday night and tell us that it was OK for the coming Sunday because nobody would be on duty. We had a clear run. He always told us the truth.

CHAPTER TWENTY

A personal bombshell forced me to take a lesser role in the station.

I am not a great believer in conspiracy theories but there was a series of possibly unconnected occurrences that ended with my life being turned upside down.

First of all, I noticed that there seemed to be an unusual amount of engineering activity on the Post Office telephone distribution box that was outside my house. For many days and at strange times, this man was sitting, working on the box.

It was also at this time that I started to get strange 'clicks' on my telephone. I put it down initially to having a party line. This was common practice in the 1970s where two completely different households shared a single phone line. If they were making a call, then I couldn't and if I was making a call then they couldn't.

I was sufficiently concerned about these 'clicks' that I insisted that nothing strategic should be discussed with me over this phone; especially the location of the following Sunday's broadcast.

Then the doorbell rang one evening and there was a 'market researcher' standing outside wanting to interview me on my views about politics and current affairs. If the Post Office had approached MI5 to send one of their 'spooks' to do this interview, then she would have been exactly the sort of person I would have expected to see. She was powerful, self-assured and an excellent interviewer. Perhaps I should have refused but the opportunity to discuss politics and current affairs was too much to resist: too flattering.

I remember thinking to myself that she could be dangerous and therefore made sure to present myself as a very reasonable person with no particular leaning towards any political party.

I also remember being asked my views on the Monarchy and expressing my view that the beauty of a constitutional Monarchy was, 'It was not the power that the Queen holds but the power that she stops other people from holding.' I don't think she was expecting that response.

She was with me for more than an hour and then she left. We never discussed radio and she certainly made no attempt at any sort of 'product placement', which is what I would have expected from a 'market researcher'. She would have gleaned a pretty accurate idea of my lifestyle and attitudes. She would also have gained a good indication of my areas of vulnerability.

I had been working during the day as a salesman in the grocery trade. Suddenly, Eric Gotts started referring to me as 'Mr Weetabix'. I found this vaguely amusing because I had never worked for that company but he was close. However, on reflection, this had to be because he had been investigating my background.

One evening, I was staying in a hotel in Bournemouth, when I received a phone call from my boss, asking to me to meet him at Dorking Station, the following morning.

He looked serious. It transpired that someone from the Post Office had been to see him and informed him of my involvement with Radio Kaleidoscope. There are no prizes for guessing who it was! The result was that I was summarily dismissed and, with no chance of a reference, it was going to be extremely difficult to get back into my chosen profession. Any attempt to get back into employment was likely to be met with the same sort of visit to my 'would-be' bosses.

Suddenly, I had become one of Brian's 'dummies'. Financially, this could not have come at a worse moment. In one very smart move, I had been blown right out of the picture and onto the sidelines. I needed to rethink my life and my means of earning a living. The only safe way was to become self-employed. The question was, in what sort of business should I become self-employed?

Whilst I rebuilt my life, I had to take a back-seat.

It had often been discussed amongst ourselves but now we all agreed that the logical way forward was to join forces with Radio Jackie.

The merger was remarkably easy and amicable. As Maurice had put it so eloquently:-

'Jackie was a cause – Kaleidoscope was a sound.'

Radio Jackie was already trying to sound like Kaleidoscope. We had succeeded in getting our first imitator.

We could keep up the non-stop music radio sound that was so original when we started but we could drive it forward so much better when combined with the idealism that was Radio Jackie.

Jackie only ever wanted to provide a local radio service to South West London and North Surrey.

It was based around the Sutton area and the studios were at 77 Burleigh Road the home of a remarkable family: the Catfords.
Nick Catford, the son, had doggedly persisted with Radio Jackie. It was a remarkable feat of perseverance. No matter what had happened, he managed to get a signal out the following Sunday – without fail.

I had a huge respect for Nick. He was a well rounded character with wide interests. He was a talented black and white photographer, had abiding interests in potholing and underground buildings. He had a great 'ear' for music and a fabulous microphone voice. He was utterly determined to see Radio Jackie succeed.

Jack Catford, his father, was an ageing ex-rear gunner in Lancaster bombers during World War II; amazingly he had survived 60 sorties. He pretended not to notice what was going on in his house in the name of Radio Jackie but he later confided to me that, 'I did my bit for freedom during the war, now Nicholas is doing the same.' The pride was tangible. However, he was no saint. Rumour had it that he let off his service revolver during an argument with his wife, Molly. If this was true, I never saw any bullet holes in the ceiling or walls but what I did see was a genuine love for Molly and remarkable tolerance of his two sons.

However, he would proudly relate the occasion during the war when an incendiary bomb landed on his roof and failed to explode. He picked it out of the gutter and realised that it didn't have a detonator. The following night he inserted a detonator and threw it out of the window of his Lancaster whilst over Hamburg.

'I thought the bastards would like to have it back.' He chuckled with pride, in his rasping voice.

Molly Catford, Nick's mother, was inspirational. What she achieved with a smile, some encouraging words and a cup of tea (always a cup of tea) was little short of amazing. Molly had enjoyed a brief career on the stage as one of the celebrated troupe of Tiller Girls before she married Jack and had her two sons, Nick and Andy.

She positively buzzed with the excitement of Radio Jackie. She supported unquestioningly what Nick was doing. This meant that she totally accepted everyone else on Jackie. Her 'boys' as she used to call them. Above all she loved the thrill of having all her 'boys' around her. She was a 'mother' to all of them and they loved her in return.

To knock on the door of 77 Burleigh Road was to be greeted by the most welcoming smile anyone could wish for, followed by, 'Hello – do come in – would you like a cup of tea?'

Molly's cups of tea healed many arguments, resolved innumerable problems and held Radio Jackie together.

Having said that, she was not averse to storming into the local police station and demanding back equipment, which had been confiscated earlier in the day. She would emerge triumphant with transmitters, cassette recorders, car batteries and load them into a waiting car.

Being a land-based pirate was not glamorous particularly on a cold, wet, Sunday in January, when the rain had been dripping down your neck and you were soaked through. The signal had not got out well and to top it all, Eric Gotts had turned up with the police and grabbed all the equipment.

It was days like these when Molly truly shone.

'Now boys, let's all have a cup of tea.' The mandatory cuppa.

'Have we got a transmitter for next week?' Then...

'Now where shall we broadcast from next week?' Followed by...

'When do you want to come round here and record your programmes?'

We always left fully recovered and ready for the following Sunday.

MP in tune with much-raided Radio Jackie

EPSOM AND EWELL's MP Archie Hamilton has put his support behind Radio Jackie, the Surrey and South London pirate radio station.

For nine years, a band of men and women have kept the station going despite repeated raids by police and Post Office.

Now two of the radio's workers have visited Mr Hamilton at his surgery in a bid to get him on their wave-length.

Mr Hamilton said later: "This is a technical issue and will have to be carefully considered. But I must say that I found their case persuasive.

"And I find the idea of community radio along the lines they suggest quite appealing.

"I am seeking information from the Home Office and I am also trying to find out the position my party take on this.

"If I find that it is technically possible to have such stations, but attitudes are still against them, then I may well take up the issue in the Commons myself."

Radio Jackie broadcasts on Sundays on 227 metres on the medium wave band at power of 50 watts. It caters for Sutton, Epsom, Croydon, Leatherhead, Wandsworth and Streatham — but can be received over much of South London.

As soon as transmission starts the crew begins a cat-and-mouse game with police.

Programme controller Nick Catford, of Sutton, said: "We are having a lot of trouble at the moment. We are raided regularly and equipment has been seized.

"We feel we have the enthusiasm to run Radio Jackie as a full-time community station — provided we are given a chance."

Epsom and Ewell Herald 1978

To Molly, her 'boys' could do no wrong. Even if they had! There had been frequent appearances in the local Magistrates' Court on charges of illegal broadcasting. This, of course, was duly reported in the local press, the *Sutton Advertiser*.

To keep up the pretence that her husband Jack did not know what was going on, she would cut out the offending articles from the paper.

Frequently, we would see Jack peering through the holes in the *Advertiser*. Whenever he queried this, Molly assured him that she had cut out a coupon that she wanted.

Jack was no fool.
One of the Radio Jackie 'team' was a young lad called Kevin Stewart. At the time he had "no fixed abode". He broadcast under the name of Tony Bond and had a very pleasing voice and manner. He was a natural for radio.

Molly always looked after her 'boys' and Kevin was no exception. Particularly because of his plight, he brought out her strong maternal instincts. Kevin often said that she was more of a mother to him than his own mother.

Kevin would stay late at Burleigh Road until Jack would stretch his arms in his armchair and yawn and announce, 'Molly, I think shall head off to bed. Will you be long?'

'I'll just say goodbye to Kevin and then I shall be up.'

He climbed the stairs

Molly would then pull out a pillow and some blankets and make up a bed on the sofa. She wanted to make sure that Kevin had a roof over his head for the night.

The following morning, she would wake up to the alarm, race downstairs and usher Kevin out of the front door.

Half an hour later, Kevin would ring on the front doorbell.

'I wonder who that could be?' Molly would express surprise. She would get up from the breakfast table and open the door.

'Oh Kevin! How lovely to see you.'

Then theatrically to Jack, 'Oh, Jack, why - it's Kevin!'

'Do come in. Have you had any breakfast?'

This little charade was repeated every day, for many months. I feel it says much about the big-hearted character of the man because Jack never said anything and Jack really was no fool.

Kevin, today, is the Chief Executive of the Tindle Radio Group, in charge of fifteen radio stations.

CHAPTER TWENTY-ONE

It was dark and we were up on Epsom Downs overlooking the whole of London. It was a lovely sight with all the lights of the big city twinkling away in front of us.

Nick had made the decision to expand our broadcasting to weekday evenings on FM because it was so much easier to achieve. We retained Medium Wave for our Sunday broadcasts.

Transmitting on FM was simple because it only required an aerial similar to a television aerial, which was pointing from high ground towards London. Epsom Downs was perfect.

We had found the perfect tree to install the aerial and Tony Collis had shinned up and positioned it. The problem was that the tree was in someone's back garden.

It was dark, nobody was watching, so we went ahead with the broadcast. We took immense care not to cause any damage. It would have given us extremely bad publicity if we had.

Near this tree was a greenhouse and a shed. For some reason, the owner of the house had left a bowler hat on one of the shelves.

The signal was getting out well and we were getting good reports back from Maggie who was manning the phone line.

Suddenly Brian Horne hissed, 'Police, get away! Just go.'

We looked up and saw two policemen walking up the garden path.

We scattered. There was no time to collect the transmitter, it was every man for himself.

Except Brian.

Brian coolly walked over to the shelf and picked up the bowler hat and put it on his head. Then he walked out to meet the two policemen.

'My that was quick, officer!' He politely tapped the brim of the bowler hat and the policemen responded by touching the peaks of their caps.

'Now quickly, there were three of them. Two went in that direction and the other went down the hill. Hurry! They are less than a minute away!'

The policemen both jumped over the fence and raced away.

Brian carefully replaced the hat on the shelf and walked calmly down the front drive and out of the gate onto the street beside the police car and away.

We waited half an hour and then cautiously slipped back and collected all the equipment.

We decided not to broadcast from that site again.

In fact, we did broadcast from very near to this house, about two weeks later. It was round to the back of the Derby Arms pub on Epsom Downs on a Thursday evening. It was getting dark and the broadcast was getting out well.

Suddenly, we spotted the Post Office detector van. It was a Ford Transit with a large extendable aerial, like a huge pole sticking out of the roof.

Brian walked over towards the van. He always tried to engage them in conversation because it delayed them and gave us more time on air and also bought more time to escape. In this case, back into the Derby Arms.

Post Office detector van

The detector van was stationary whilst they were pinpointing exactly where we were. They had not seen Brian approaching.

At that moment a police car pulled up alongside Brian. He assumed, because Brian was wearing a suit, that he was from the Post Office detection team.

'I assume that's them over there?' the policeman said to Brian, pointing to the van with the tall pole sticking out of the roof. It was a commonly held belief that Radio Jackie broadcast from a van whilst driving around.

'Yes,' he replied. 'They are so blatant these days.'

'So this Radio Jackie broadcasts from that van, does it?'
'Yes and the cheek of it is they've stuck Post Office labels on the side of the van. It certainly fools most people.'

The policeman paused, 'What are these guys like?'

'Oh, they are OK, but don't believe a word they say. These guys would sell their own grandmothers.'

The policeman and Brian nodded a mutual understanding.

Then Brian added, 'You'd better go over there and arrest them, but you want to make sure you smell the smoke coming from their cigarettes. I'll bet it's highly dodgey – you know what I mean.' Brian tapped the side of his nose, knowingly.

The policeman nodded.

He thanked Brian and swung into action. Tonight he was not only going to catch a radio pirate but get a drugs 'bust' at the same time.

Brian retreated to a safe distance and got the message back to us to be ready to run. We waited... and waited.

Eventually, the policeman emerged from the detector van and climbed back into his car and ostentatiously escorted the van down the road and off to Epsom Police Station to check out their story. I would have loved to have been a fly on the wall.

The whole broadcast went out that night.

CHAPTER TWENTY-TWO

It was the middle of August and there was another Free Radio Rally being held in Trafalgar Square.

We decided that Radio Jackie had to broadcast to the rally. The problem was where to find a transmitting site in central London that would have thundered out at the rally?

Houses were OK but you could rarely get the correct length aerial or get it high enough. This meant a greatly reduced signal.

Tony Collis was always asking for height and what he called the perfect 'quarter-wave aerial' - 200 feet straight up.

Tony's obsession with height would get me frantic with fear and worry on many occasions.

To rig an aerial, Tony would climb a very tall tree. This could be 60, 70 or even 80 feet above the ground. He would grab the wire, some string and an insulator and shin up the tree.

Tony, climbing the main part of the tree, rarely bothered me. It was when he got to the top.

'Wow Tony, that is really high. No need to go any higher. Tie it there.'

'No, I can go up quite a bit higher.'

'Tony, be careful, I don't want to have to catch you.'

A grunt and Tony would climb up another six feet. By now the tree was about the thickness of your thumb and Tony would be swaying in all directions.

'No further Tony, that will be fine!'

**Tony Collis nears the
top of a tree**

Another grunt and he climbed another six feet. It looked hideously precarious. At that point, Tony's allergy to pine pollen would kick in and there would be a fit of sneezing.

'Aaaaaachoo! Aaaaachoo! Aaaachoo!'

I would stand on the ground, helpless; waiting for Tony to come crashing through the branches. Should I try to catch him or would that simply kill us both? I never worked out an answer and thankfully Tony never gave me cause to.

Tony was, and is, totally fearless. Somehow he always knew just how far he could go. So when Tony suggested height for the broadcast to the rally, we looked at the rows of houses in Notting Hill and thought they are only 50 feet high, maximum.

Then I followed his eyes to a tall block of luxury flats. Brian Horne and I gazed at the building. This would make a perfect location. There was even a suitable bit of cover to be had in the waste land that was on the other side of the road to the building.

'How high do you think it is?' I asked.

Brian and Tony started counting the number of storeys. It was perfect. The problem, however, was getting past the security guards on the main reception.

Brian and I went back home, changed into our suits and filled my briefcase with the aerial, string and insulator. Then we returned.

Tony waited outside whilst Brian and I wandered into the foyer.

We were earnestly talking as we passed the security guards. Brian nodded diffidently towards them and they nodded back. We were through. Into the lift. Up to the top floor. Out and up onto the roof. Wow! It was high.

We carefully lowered the aerial wire over the side and down to Tony who caught hold of it and walked it calmly across to the waste land.

We secured our end and caught the lift down to the ground. We were still in earnest conversation as we walked out of the door and away.

It was an exposed site to transmit from but it was fantastic for the rally. It was the strongest signal on the band. In fact it was perhaps the strongest signal we ever managed to radiate. It was so strong that the signal was picked up at a monitoring station in Glasgow.

71

CHAPTER TWENTY-THREE

When the government took the responsibility for tracking and closing illegal broadcasts away from the Post Office and handed it to the Home Office, Jim Crow, Eric Gotts and their teams went with it.

The tall, grey-haired, affable Jim Crow remained as he had always been. However, Eric Gotts took a sinister turn for the worse. It was as though he was now some Home Office commando.

The first time we noticed his change in behaviour was one evening on an FM broadcast on top of the North Downs near Caterham.

We had a lovely view of London and the broadcast was going brilliantly. It was a moonless night; a warm and pleasant evening.

Brian Horne had a high-powered flashlight. To call it a torch would be wrong. We were cursing him because every time he turned it on it ruined our night vision. He seemed oblivious to this, stabbing the beam hither and thither.

Eric Gotts and his team were wearing camouflage clothing and crawling along the ground towards our site. They were only thirty feet away, having worked their way past all our security, when Brian's beam landed full on them.

Chaos broke out. Lights, torches, whistles, shouts, yells – it was pandemonium. The Gotts team leapt to their feet and ran straight for the transmitter.

I was standing beside the prized box so did the only thing I could. I grabbed it and ran blindly into the night and away from the approaching torches.

I remember running totally blind. I bounced into and around trees, I crashed through undergrowth. Everything was pitch black. I couldn't see where I was running. I just knew I had to get the transmitter as far away as possible before hiding it.

My head lolled back, my sightless eyes wide, my mouth open. I realised exactly what it was like to be totally blind. It was not a pleasant experience.

I ran and ran. Suddenly there was nothing beneath my feet and I was falling. I held onto the transmitter but being blind made me helpless and perhaps that is what saved me.

I had run off the top of one of those cliffs, that you can now see from the M25, on the south side of the North Downs.
Helplessly, I dropped onto a large bush or a tree. It hurt and I was winded but I was not injured.

I lay there gasping for breath and trying to make sense of what had happened and where I was.

I must have lain there for several minutes before I attempted to climb down the tree that I had never climbed up. I had no clue how high up I was or what lay in store for me at the bottom. It was so dark.

Gradually my eyes accustomed themselves a bit and I could make out the faint outline of the cliff. I could also see vaguely that the tree was not that high and that it was growing out of the side of the cliff.

Fortunately for me it was not a vertical cliff. Also I was fortunate in that it was a chalk cliff which showed white, even when there was no moonlight. I climbed down clutching my precious box.

The tree was growing out of a ledge in the cliff and as I peered into the darkness, I could see a black stripe against the white. I prayed that the ledge would lead me back onto the hillside.

It wasn't easy. The ledge was narrow and also crumbled quite a bit. I was a pretty panicky by this time. I set off along the ledge and soon made it to the side of the cliff and onto the hillside.

It was still very dark and I blundered my way to where I thought the road would be. I recall tripping over a couple in an advanced state of undress. It was a warm night and this was a well known spot for courting couples. They cursed me and I said, 'Ooops sorry,' and continued on until I reached the road.

A car soon picked me up and we made our way off to the pub.

Eric Gotts had 'upped his game'. He had always been nasty, now he was getting very nasty.

CHAPTER TWENTY-FOUR

If you had looked towards Crystal Palace from anywhere in London, the two most visible things you would have seen were the transmitting masts. The biggest belonged to the BBC and broadcast their television signal. It was very high and gave excellent coverage of the whole of the Greater London area.

Close to this mast was another, slightly smaller mast at Beulah Hill. This belonged to the IBA and broadcast ITV.

Capital Radio and LBC were soon to be launched and we had learned that the aerials were going to be placed at the top of the Beulah Hill mast.

I remember looking at the mast wistfully and saying, 'Wouldn't it be brilliant if we could transmit from that mast too.'

Brian smiled and I thought nothing more about it.

Then about four weeks later, we all gathered one evening for one of our regular broadcasts, when Brian explained that we were going to be broadcasting from a rather special site.

The IBA mast at Beulah Hill

We piled into three vehicles and drove off in the direction of Beulah Hill. Brian stopped us at the foot of the main mast and got out of his van.

'Bloody Hell Brian, we can't broadcast from here! We'll get nicked.'

Brian smiled knowingly. There was a public lavatory close to the foot of the mast and near that was a fence.

'I'm not going over that fence, Brian. It's too risky.'

There was a general murmur of disquiet from everyone and a couple of guys made to head off back to the cars.

'You don't have to.' He smiled triumphantly. He looked down.

At his feet was a coil of thick, heavy duty coaxial cable. My eyes followed it through a gap in the fence and then straight up the mast.

'I've a friend of mine, who works for the IBA. He told me that the aerial is in place at the top of the mast and this is the coaxial cable that they, the engineers, will connect to the new Capital Radio transmitter, tomorrow. Tonight it is just lying here begging to be used.'

'So you climbed over the fence and got it?'
'No,' replied Brian. 'My friend pushed it through.'

He then bent down and picked up the end of the cable and showed us the connector that he had fitted earlier.

We all looked at each other. This was going to be risky and we would be in trouble if we got caught. However, it was a once in a lifetime chance to get Radio Jackie coming from the best point in the whole of London.

We switched on. 'Love Theme' blasted out of our radios. It was the strongest signal we had ever managed to put out.

We had four hours of programmes prepared for that night and none of us thought we would last an hour. We were decidedly edgy.

We tucked the equipment into a bush by the fence and covered everything up so that nothing was visible. Then we took up our lookout duties.

It was near the end of the second hour that Jim Crow and his small team were first spotted. They seemed confused.

'I think the height of the aerial is confusing them. Don't switch anything off, let's just watch,' whispered Brian.

They walked up and down several times and then returned to their van. The detection aerials were turning this way and that.

Then they got out of the van again and walked straight past our transmitter. Looking. Searching.

Jim looked up at the mast on several occasions but then resumed his tracking efforts with his specially adapted radio receiver.

None of us moved. We had all hidden in the shadows and in the dark we could scarcely see much of what was going on. We hardly dared to breathe.

At the end of the third hour, Jim and his team had wandered away. So Brian smartly went over to the transmitter and inserted the tape for the fourth hour.

He disappeared into the shadows again.
Jim and his team walked round and round but were obviously getting nowhere in their search.

We watched and held our breath. They came and they went. They produced torches and flashed them in all directions.They were concentrating on the trees. It was a sensible guess on their part because almost every other broadcast we had made had come from a tree somewhere in South West London.

When the final hour finished, Jim was well away from the transmitter, so we quickly switched off and put the equipment into one of the cars and away it went.

**Brian Horne and Paul Lock packing up after
the Beulah Hill broadcast**

Brian, meanwhile produced a screwdriver and calmly removed his connector on the end of the coaxial cable and then carefully stuffed the full coil back through the fence.

'I'm not losing that connector,' he declared. 'It's a good one.'

The following afternoon, Jim Crow rang Brian. 'Say Brian, that was a very good signal you were putting out last night.'

'Aah,' said Brian knowingly.

'We couldn't get a fix on you. We reckoned you were coming from pretty high up. Where were you?"

'Aah,' said Brian. 'Now that would be telling.'

CHAPTER TWENTY-FIVE

The M25, when it was under construction, provided us with some wonderful transmitting sites, especially for the night time FM service.

A motorway is an amazing feat of engineering and, unbeknown to most people, it has an impressive drainage system. Huge concrete pipework designed to cope with almost anything that the weather can throw at it. It's the reason that you get surface water on motorways but they rarely flood.

One evening, the aerial was up a tree close to the edge of the new motorway construction site. There were pipes piled high about a couple of hundred yards away and it was obvious that work was going on, during the day, to connect and bury these drains.

Not far from where we were transmitting, there was an access manhole, several feet across, that had just been built. It was covered with a sheet of corrugated iron.

Tony walked over to it and had a close look. 'We must be careful not to step on that. We could fall quite a long way down.'

We always had a respect for the construction work so it was no issue staying away from the manhole.

The transmission had been going out for a couple of hours when we suddenly looked up and saw Jim Crow standing beside us.

'I'm sorry guys but you're all nicked!'

Brian started to talk his way out of the situation but it was even beyond him.

Jim picked up the transmitter and began to walk away. He turned and looked over his shoulder and said, 'I really do have every scrap of evidence I need to make a case stand up in court. I repeat, YOU'RE ALL NICKED.'

At that moment there was a crash and a thump followed by a loud grunt of pain. In the dark, he had stepped on the corrugated iron sheet and had fallen down the manhole. He was quite a way down and Jim was a man in his fifties. He was not going to get out without help.

'HELP ME!'

If it had been Eric Gotts, we would have left him there, but we couldn't find it in ourselves to do that to Jim.

We all rushed over and peered down the hole. Jim's glasses glinted in the moonlight. 'Please help me out guys?'

'Have you damaged the transmitter?' It was Tony.

'No I think it's OK.'

'Well I think you ought to pass it up to me first of all.'

Pause

Then Brian chipped in, 'It's a Friday night, Jim, work won't start again here until Monday. Would you like me to bring you some sandwiches?'

'No Brian, get me out of here.'

'But Jim, you said you had all the evidence for a conviction. Now we all need to think about that, don't we?'

Jim grunted.

'Now Jim, if we help you out of there, are we still all nicked?'

'OK, Brian. Please help me out of here?'

78

Tony chirped, 'I think you should pass us the transmitter first, don't you?'

There was a pause, then something moved and Jim held the precious transmitter above his head. Tony grabbed hold of it and passed it to Brian. Within seconds it was in a car and being driven away at speed.

'Come on Jim, give us your hands.'

We all leaned over the edge and reached down and grabbed at his hands and arms. He was a dead weight because he was unable to help us but we swiftly hauled him out of the manhole. He sat down on a concrete slab and rubbed his shin.

Jim Crow

Brian flashed his torch at it. It was bleeding but not seriously. He had had a lucky escape.

We took him down to the Happy Eater at Betchworth and bought him a cup of tea and made sure he was OK.

That was the nearest we ever came to losing an FM transmitter.

CHAPTER TWENTY-SIX

Janet Street-Porter, for the London Today programme on ITV came with us for one of our Sunday medium wave transmissions. She was recording a story about us and wanted to film us going about our work.

This could have been terrific publicity and we were keen to appear as professional and polished as possible. It was important that nothing went wrong (or at least was seen to go wrong!)

We set up a good site near Walton on the Hill, which we hoped would impress her.

The ITV Film Unit

She was getting some excellent shots of us setting up and switching on when about a hundred yards away we noticed a man with a dog, heading in our direction.

We didn't want Janet Street-Porter to record any of our 'look-out' activities. We were also anxious for her not to realise anything was wrong.

Brian strode out towards the man. 'What are you doing on my land?'

'It's OK, I'm an off-duty police officer and I thought I saw some suspicious activity so I am investigating.'

'Well, not here you're not. This is my land I can do what I please here. Go and investigate somewhere else.'

To our amazement, he apologised and turned round and walked away.

The filming continued. We were beginning to relax when another man appeared in the distance.

Again Brian went out to meet him. Before he could lay ownership to the land, the man said, 'What are you doing on my neighbour's field?'

Brian calmly pointed to the 200 feet of aerial wire, stretching away into the trees and said. 'We are recording 'bird song'.'

'Oh!' said the man. 'Isn't that Janet Street-Porter?'

'Yes, she's very interested in the wildlife.' Brian was gaining in confidence. 'She does a lot of walking too.'

The man took another couple of steps forward.

Brian held his hand out. 'Do you mind, this equipment is very sensitive, it picks up the faintest noise. Please don't go any closer.' He raised his finger to his mouth, 'Ssssh!'

The two watched for a couple more minutes then he whispered, 'I'll creep away then.' Brian nodded.

Janet Street-Porter and her cameraman were blissfully unaware of what was going on.

Shortly afterwards, she announced that she had all the footage they needed and, wishing us well, they both left.

No sooner had she gone than Eric Gotts swooped. We had relaxed our guard for a few moments and he had caught us.

Soon we were standing by the road with the transmitter, car battery, inverter, and cassette recorder, lined up against the hedge.

'Where are you taking the kit, Eric?' asked Tony.

"Down to Caterham Police Station."

'Can we come too?'

Tony and Brian followed Eric Gotts and walked into the Police Station with him. Tony and Brian were protesting loudly that Eric had stolen their equipment. Eric was shouting at them to be quiet. The desk sergeant was shouting at everyone to be quiet. It was a moment of chaos.

Eric Gotts stepped forward and pulled the policeman to one side. 'I work for the Home Office and here is my identification. Can I have a quick word with you?'

For a few seconds, they had their back turned to the equipment.

81

Brian smartly reached forward and removed the fuse in the transmitter and replaced it with another much weaker one.

Eric and the desk sergeant turned back.

'I'm confiscating this equipment.'

'Not without a confiscation order you don't,' said Tony.
They looked at each other. 'Pass me a phone, I'll ring through to get one.'

Brian looked them both straight in the eyes, 'What exactly do you think you are confiscating?'

'Don't come any of your rubbish, Brian. This is a working transmitter and I have the powers to have this confiscated.' Then with glee, he added. 'You're nicked and you know it.'

'But it's not a working transmitter.'

Gotts hesitated. 'What do you mean?'

'This is not a working transmitter and if you confiscate it, you will be guilty of theft.'

There was a pause. 'Go on Eric, connect it up and see if it works.'

They all turned and looked at the desk sergeant.

The policeman was now in a bit of a quandary. Home Office, transmitters, theft, this was all getting out of hand.

'This is simple,' said Brian. 'I won't go anywhere near the equipment. Now if Mr Gotts here can make it work, then he can have it. But if he can't and he takes it away, it will be theft and you, officer, will be compliant.'

Another pause.

The policeman looked at Eric Gotts. 'Can you make it work?'

'Of course I can, it's simple.'

He connected the equipment up and switched on. Straight away the fuse blew.

'There you are...' said Brian. 'It's not a working transmitter, so I insist on having it back and taking it away with me. It's my equipment and this man has no right to steal it from me.'

The policeman looked across at Eric Gotts for guidance. Eric shrugged and nodded resignedly.

'All right.' The policeman reached for a large book and recorded the names of everyone and the details of what had happened.

Then Tony and Brian gathered up all the equipment, placed it into the back of Brian's van and drove away.

Eric turned to the policeman, 'You did get the number of the van, didn't you?'

CHAPTER TWENTY-SEVEN

Life in Radio Jackie was not all running away from the authorities. We certainly knew how to enjoy ourselves.

If you spend a whole day in the open air, especially with the added whiff of danger, then by the evening, you feel tired but exhilarated.

Sometimes we would go back to the Wimpy Bar in Morden but usually we finished up at the Kings Arms at Hampton Court.

It was a lovely old pub with a huge Royal crest on the front. You could park your car outside and simply walk in.

It had a slightly genteel feel to the place with wonderful oak panelling, a huge overbearing

Relaxing at the King's Arms, Hampton Court

dark oak bar. There was always a fire in the winter and above this was a pair of crossed swords. It was a lovely pub to meet in and relax and let off steam.

The owner of the Kings Arms, knew exactly who we were and was highly supportive.

Just inside the door of the bar was a huge, square, wooden table with large iron nails ostentatiously covering much of the table's surface. This was 'our' table. We could all sit around this and chat and drink and be very, very happy.

One evening, Tony Collis pulled on his pint of Ruddles and with a contented sigh announced that it was, 'a tough life being a pirate.' We laughed.

'PIRATES? PIRATES? Do I hear 'ee say there be pirates?' It was Brian Horne in his best 'Treasure Island' accent. He had leapt to the fireplace and grabbed one of the swords and was now flourishing it with great gusto.

Tony leapt up and grabbed the other sword. 'Verily you speak the truth, but who do you be?'

'I have taken the King's shilling and I have to rid this world of those dastardly varlets.'

Crash.

The swords clashed as Tony and Brian squared up. Brian, by now was up on the table. We were all howling with laughter. Then they both stood on the table, swords clashing. Tony leapt to another table and Brian followed.

'You be fleeing from the King's man, you lily-livered land-lubber. Come here and I'll run you through with this sword.' They clashed some more. Then Tony made a dash for the garden out at the back of the pub. Brian followed and so did we all.

The swords clashed some more before Tony made a leap over the back fence, straight into the Hampton Court Maze that backs onto the King's Arms.

Brian immediately followed. 'I'll get 'ee you varlet.'

84

The Maze had long since closed to the public for the night, so we all clambered over the back fence and ran around the maze, 'Hunting for Pirates'.

I occasionally caught a glimpse of Brian or Tony, swords in hand, stalking each other. The rest of us spread out across the maze, calling out that 'We all be pirates and the King's man had best beware.' We even threatened to play him a record next week.

Gradually we all drifted back into the pub and soon Tony and Brian returned, laughing and sweating profusely. They laid their weapons on the table and returned to their pints.

The landlord was thoroughly enjoying our escapades. He loved a bit of 'madness' and we certainly delivered it in spades. For some reason, he decided to play some Scottish dance music. This was too much for Brian who, once again, leapt up onto the table and started dancing over the crossed swords.

We laughed and we clapped in time with the music as Brian jigged, with his arms held aloft.

Gradually we all, in turn, demonstrated our own prowess in Scottish sword dancing. Kevin Stewart, outrageous as ever, tried to do a Cossack sword dance which went well until he fell over backwards onto the table to howls of laughter.

The evening would continue in much the same way until closing time. This was the point at which, the landlord, Tony Jarvis, would gather up all the money that we had spent over the bar and hand it back to us, saying, 'Go and buy yourselves some new car batteries or equipment with this.'

He was, like so many people, a great supporter of Radio Jackie.

CHAPTER TWENTY-EIGHT

It was like the opening sequence of 'Porridge'.

'Nicholas Catford, you are an habitual offender for whom a fine holds no fears. I therefore have no alternative but to sentence you to a term of imprisonment for 28 days. Take him down.'

We sat in the Magistrates' Court stunned.

'PRISON!'

Somebody shouted, 'Prison, just for entertaining the public?'

Nick looked shaken. He had not expected this but then neither had any of us. He was led away and we gathered outside the court. We were thunderstruck.

How could we go on?

Eric Gotts had made a brilliant case against Nick and he smirked with satisfaction as he emerged from the court.

Molly, Nick's mother, was there too. 'Well boys, let's all go and have a cup of tea.'

A stunned group outside court

We trooped forlornly back to 77 Burleigh Road and Molly put the kettle on.

'Now boys, have we got a transmitter for next Sunday?'

Tony nodded.

'Which site are we going to use?'

'Beddington Sewage Farm.' It was Tony again.

'Now Nick is not going to be able to make his programme, is he? So who is going to do it?' Molly beamed bravely round to everyone. Her son had gone to prison just an hour before and here she was, holding Radio Jackie together, single-handed.

Gradually the mood improved.

'I think another cup of tea is called for.'

CHAPTER TWENTY-NINE

As each week passed, Eric Gotts became bolder. Camouflage, stealth, and confiscation were becoming the pattern. We were on the run and Eric Gotts was leading the charge.

Eric Gotts trying not to be photographed

In one of our conversations with Jim Crow, he revealed that Eric was now a man consumed with a passion for finally closing Radio Jackie.

Now it was personal.

Nick emerged from prison a chastened man. It had not been a pleasant experience for him and it was obvious that it was one that he did not wish to repeat. However, he still ran Radio Jackie and Molly supported him unswervingly.

It was agreed that for a while, at least, Nick should not stay with the transmitter but should join the group providing the security. Nick seemed content with that.

It worked well and soon Jackie was back on track although the raids were becoming more frequent.

One momentous Sunday saw another raid. Eric Gotts was leading the attack and he chased and caught up with Dave Owen and the transmitter before it could be hidden.

A struggle ensued as Eric tried to confiscate it. Then he rained a series of blows down upon Dave.

The scenario changed at that moment.

Up until then, we had been peaceful. We still were. But now Gotts was becoming violent.

We handed over the transmitter, not wishing to get into a fight. He smirked and took notes of all our names and marched away.

Tony Collis was incensed, 'He can't be allowed to get away with that.'

Even Molly acknowledged that the situation was becoming 'thuggish' and it wasn't coming from our side.

Something had to be done. Tony marched into the nearest police station and made a formal complaint. They had to act.

Tony consulted a solicitor and Eric Gotts was sued for common assault.

The raids stopped whilst the court action was pending.

Eric Gotts and the Home Office mounted an impressive defence in which they claimed that there had been an affray and that Gotts was the innocent victim of an assault. However, nobody could deny the fact that blows had been struck, that Eric Gotts had been the attacker and that there were many witnesses.

Eric Gotts was found GUILTY.

The Home Office appealed but that failed too.

The man now had a criminal record.

We only saw Eric Gotts once more and much later.

CHAPTER THIRTY

There were no more raids after the court case. The Eric Gotts incident had had a salutary effect upon the rest of the Home Office team. They obviously did not want to get criminal records too.

There followed a 'phoney war'.

We broadcast for several Sundays without a raid. We had no idea what they were thinking. Jim Crow was not telling us what was happening although he made it abundantly clear that there was not going to be a raid each time we asked.

He was, as always, true to his word. We had known Jim for many years and this was where the change happened. In the beginning we were just youngsters, teenagers, playing 'cops and robbers'. True the real fun was in radio but there was always the thrill of the chase.

We had grown up; some of us were in our thirties. Tony Collis was in his mid twenties, a mature man with a thriving business that he had developed himself from the fruit machines that he had taken apart and repaired in his bedroom all those years before.

Tony Collis, by his own admission, has a very short attention span. But for once he settled down and applied himself to the next stage of Radio Jackie.

He read, re-read and thoroughly digested the 'Wireless Telegraphy Act'. This was the only legislation that concerned Radio Jackie and the Home Office. It spelt out exactly what they could do and, by omission, what they could not.

As it transpired, the Act was incredibly weak and poorly drafted. It was obviously written for a time before there were pirates.

Tony Collis

The only powers that the Home Office officials had were to turn off the transmitter. They had no powers of confiscation. The only offence was 'not to turn off the transmitter', when asked.

In other words, Tony concluded, 'There is nothing stopping us from broadcasting 24 hours a day.'

'We simply broadcast until the Home Office arrives. When they ask us to turn off the transmitter, we do just that. Then when they have gone, we turn it back on again and carry on. That way we are totally within the law.'

We continued in this way for some time as gradually the number of 'raids' reduced.

The Home Office had obviously realised that they had insufficient 'teeth' and that Radio Jackie was 'running rings around it'.

CHAPTER THIRTY-ONE

The next phase of Radio Jackie began the following Christmas. We were broadcasting from the old Tate & Lyle building in Wandsworth. Tony was convinced that the time had arrived to test the government's resolve.

The Wireless Telegraphy Act gave no right of confiscation to the Home Office so Tony decided the next raid was going to be the test.

Christmas was always the time when Jim Crow, Eric Gotts and their teams spent time with their families and left the airwaves to us.

Christmas Day merged into Boxing Day. As expected, there was no raid. So we carried on broadcasting. The response from the listeners was phenomenal. They knew what we were doing and loved it.

The day after Boxing Day, the Home Office van pulled up outside the old Tate & Lyle building and moved in to grab the equipment. Tony argued that they had no right of confiscation but they took the equipment anyway.

Tony and Dave Owen followed them back to Wandsworth Police Station, whereupon they both walked in and demanded a return of the transmitters. Tony waved his copy of the Wireless Telegraphy Act and quoted the exact wording.

There was nothing that the police or the Home Office could do. So lamely they handed back all of the equipment.

Tony and Dave drove back to the old Tate & Lyle building and reinstalled the transmitter. We were back on the air within quarter of an hour.

The Home Office now realised that they had a serious problem with us. The Act was too weak and gave them little authority. Hence there was nothing stopping us from broadcasting round the clock.

However, to take it to a 24/7 operation required guts, organisation and money. People were going to have to give up their jobs to do programmes and sell advertising.

Programmes were going to have to be 'live'. We couldn't pre-record them any more. Somebody had to sell advertising. Somebody had to make sure the adverts were played at the right time. Somebody had to keep the accounts.

The lads who had 'larked around' pushing transmitters in prams all those years ago now had a serious business to run. We were suddenly faced with being a very real radio station.

It was the 'lad' who showed me his fruit machines in his bedroom on our first meeting who proved to be our salvation: Tony Collis.

Tony's fruit machine business was more than thriving. It was providing him with a highly profitable income.

So he put to the Radio Jackie team an ultimatum. He would 'back' the station with his own money but he had to be the sole owner. He would take the risk but he would also take any profits. Nobody was in a position to argue. Besides, nobody would have wanted to argue. The dream was coming true. The future looked exciting yet uncertain but we still couldn't be confident that the Home Office wouldn't find some way of stopping us.

We could not stay in Wandsworth forever, we had to find a new more permanent location.

We could no longer run aerials up trees. This was because the transmitter would be out in the open and too vulnerable. What was needed was a secure shed at the bottom of a garden.

Dave Owen's mother came to the rescue here. She lived in Abbotts Road, just off the Sutton By-pass. It was the perfect position for getting the signal into the target service area of Sutton, Kingston, Wimbledon, Croydon and Epsom.

A high mast was rigged at the bottom of the garden and the aerial slung from that towards the house. The transmitter was in the shed, which until then had been Dave's studio.

The Radio Jackie aerial in Abbotts Road, Sutton

However, this studio was not the solution to generating the programmes.

Tony appointed Dave Owen as Programme Controller. He was the obvious choice.

The problem was where to have the studios and also, if the studios were not beside the transmitter, how to link the two together.

Eddie Couzens, a highly supportive listener, offered Tony, on a purely pay-as-you-go rental, a flat in Joanna House over a shop just off Central Road, Worcester Park.

Later we had to move to larger premises. Eddie Couzens offered us another flat around the corner and this was where we stayed. The address was 32a Central Road. It was ideal for our purposes because it could only be reached through the front door and up a steep flight of stairs. A raid could be held at bay for some time.

The flat was on two floors. The main office was on the first floor and the studios were on the second.

The connection to the transmitter was via a UHF radio link.

We carried on broadcasting. Days became weeks. Nothing. Nobody tried to stop us.

We plunged into Monday and soon it was Tuesday and before we knew it, it was the weekend again and still nobody tried to stop us.

So a couple of weeks became a month.

The serious business of running a radio station had started.

Dave Owen as Programme Controller was looking for people who would regularly do shows – for free. Tony was taking a big risk with his money so anything that could keep costs down had to be welcomed.

Gradually characters started to emerge. The charismatic Roger Mowbray brought his own inimitable style to the station. His quirky sense of humour and style of delivery soon caught on with the listeners.

Another young aspiring man was Paul McKenna, who later became the celebrated TV hypnotist. He also had a regular show.

Mike Hayes, one of the founders of Radio Jackie was a regular presenter. So too was Dave Cliff, who used the name Dave Stevens.

**A very young Paul McKenna
in the Jackie studio**

Above: Staff at Radio Jackie work unsocial hours for as little as 50p an hour just to get on the air. Here DJ Dave Owen chats to Bernie Simmons during his broadcast.

Right: This voice could reach two million people in South West London. Already, the station estimate they have a quarter of a million regular listeners.

'We're not pirates: we don't want to be illegal'

Dave Owen shows off the studio to Bernie Simmons in the
Wallington and Sutton Advertiser

Dave Owen was the voice of the station and he worked hard – very hard. He made all the commercials and the promotional jingles as well as doing his own show every day.

The audience reaction was rapid and very positive.

Many years before, I had talked to Tony about my theory of 'Magistrates' Music'. I told him that we wanted to make it as difficult as possible for Magistrates to want to close us down because we were playing the sort of music that they liked.

Now Tony was openly talking about 'Magistrates' Music' and between him and Dave Owen, they chose music accordingly: 'Best of the New and best of the Gold'.

Dave Owen in the Jackie studio

Radio Jackie was now up and running and providing a proper service and the audience loved it.

CHAPTER THIRTY-TWO

We had won the first battle but the war was far from over.

The first job was to make the station as widely known and as popular as possible in as short a time as possible.

The next vital job was to get the politicians on our side but this could only be achieved if we were perceived as being extensively listened to. The problem with this was if we became too popular. Then the government could not ignore us. They could decide to give us a licence but the danger was that they could feel forced to act against us. It was a high risk strategy.

We watched and waited to see what would happen. The wait was not too long.

The Home Office raided the transmitter site in Abbotts Road, Sutton. It was a careful raid with everyone making sure that nobody could possibly be accused of assault.

They walked down to the shed at the bottom of the garden and confiscated all the equipment. It was all over too quickly for Tony Collis to get there to protest.

However, Tony had brought with him the replacement transmitter and Radio Jackie was back on the air within a couple of hours.

We watched and we waited. Nothing happened for a few days.

Then there came another raid. The Home Office team arrived at Abbotts Road and marched down to the shed at the bottom of the garden again, intent on confiscation. This time Tony Collis and Dave Owen had thought through their response and they had a plan.

Dave was with the transmitter.

'Excuse me, Mr Owen, do you know who owns this transmitter?' They smirked because they knew his name and because they were sure that he would deny any knowledge of the ownership of the transmitter.

Dave surprised them all.

'Why yes,' he replied brightly. 'It's mine.'

They looked nonplussed. Nobody had ever done this to them before.

'That's fine, Mr Owen.' They hesitated. 'Can we take this equipment?'

Dave looked them straight in the eyes and said, 'NO!'

At this point Tony Collis turned up and remonstrated with them forcefully, pointing out that we were NOT interfering with aircraft or shipping. We were not doing anything to disrupt the communications of the essential services. We were on a frequency that did not interfere with any other station. Therefore there was no reason why the transmitter should be switched off.

He also pointed out that Radio Jackie really ought to have a licence because it was providing a service and was doing nothing but good.

They talked between themselves and then muttered, 'OK,' took some notes and they all shuffled away.

A month later, a summons arrived for Dave Owen to appear at Sutton Magistrates' Court in four weeks time.

There was no raid in the meantime, so Jackie stayed on the air getting stronger and stronger and picking up more and more listeners.

Tony carefully re-read the Wireless Telegraphy Act and decided upon how we should play the court action.

He built a replacement transmitter and installed it carefully, one evening, and removed all the equipment that the Home Office officials had seen.

On the day of the court hearing, Dave and Tony took the, now redundant, transmitter with them and they presented it, as evidence, to the Magistrate.

There was much debate in the courtroom about Radio Jackie and what she was trying to achieve.

Tony again floored all discussion by proving that he was not causing any interference, a fact that the Home Office officials reluctantly had to agree with.

In the end, and predictably, the Magistrate found for the Home Office and Dave was fined and the equipment was confiscated.

Radio Jackie meanwhile was still on the air using the improved replacement transmitter. The service had been uninterrupted. The listeners were blissfully unaware of what we were going through.

The next raid came a few weeks later.

Again Dave Owen was with the transmitter in the shed at the bottom of his mother's garden in Abbotts Road.

The Home Office officials arrived, pretty much as before and marched down the garden path and again demanded to know who owned the equipment. This time, they were confident that Dave would claim ownership.

'Now, Mr Owen, who owns this transmitter?'

Dave smiled sweetly and replied, 'It belongs to my girl-friend, Pearl.'

They hadn't expected that response. Tony then arrived on the scene and began arguing the case for Radio Jackie with the officials.

Finally they completed their notes and strode away.

It must have been apparent to them that they could not win this situation. Every time they raided, a different person claimed ownership. The equipment was presented in court but the Radio Jackie remained on the air with an uninterrupted service.

The law was simply not strong enough to empower them to do anything more.

So that was the last that we saw of those officials for two years.

CHAPTER THIRTY-THREE

The intervening two years were not without incident. The audience was obviously growing, judging by the responses we were getting.

Advertising revenue was coming in but the efforts were being hampered by the Home Office who, having realised they could not raid, tried a different tactic. They wrote threatening letters to all our advertisers. It worked with quite a few customers but the majority of businesses were supporting us and defied the threats. None were ever prosecuted.

Radio Jackie launched several appeals for the Royal Marsden Hospital, the world-famous cancer hospital. Substantial sums were raised and the cheques were presented by celebrities like the local 'Goon' Sir Harry Secombe, and arguably the funniest stand-up comedian of the latter half of the twentieth century, Ken Dodd. The singer of 'I Remember You-oooo', Frank Ifield also presented cheques.

Jackie gives eye unit a boost

Singer, Frank Ifield presents a cheque to the eye unit of Sutton Hospital

(Below) Harry Secombe presents a cheque to Queen Mary's Hospital

SINGING star of the 'sixties, Frank Ifield came to Sutton at the weekend to do his bit for the eye unit at Sutton Hospital.

He handed over a cheque for £2,000 collected by the local pirate station, Radio Jackie, to representatives of the eye unit.

The presentation took place at the London Transport Sports Club at London Rd, North Cheam.

The money will be used to buy vital equipment for the unit that they could not otherwise afford.

The money was raised by Radio Jackie with a variety of events from discos to a sponsored slim by one of their disc jockeys Les Adams who got his weight down from 16st 8lb to 13st 8lb.

Frank Ifield was asked to make the handover because he was recently interviewed on Radio Jackie.

Our picture shows (from left) nurses Margaret Thomas and Julie Carter with Frank Ifield and hospital consultant Melea Frangoulis. [Photo: 841706

DJs Stuart Jeffries and Jimi King are joined by Sir Harry Secombe in presenting a cheque to Queen Mary's Hospital.

On the charity channel

RADIO Jackie is always trying to help the local community and one of the best ways we can do this is by running charity appeals. In 1980 it raised £1000 for a kidney machine at St Helier Hospital and £600 for video equipment for the Linden Lodge Blind School in Wimbledon.

In March 1982 Sir Harry Secombe presented Queen Mary's Hospital for Children with a cheque for £3261 which was raised by the station and its listeners, and in 1982 Radio Jackie helped a ten year old boy who suffers from muscular dystrophy, to realise the dream of his lifetime when it raised the money to send him to Cape Canaveral to see the space shuttle launched.

By the time you read this Radio Jackie will have presented The Royal Marsden Hospital Scanner Camera Appeal with a cheque for more than £2500 raised over the last few months and we will be well into our Christmas Charity Appeal for 1983 — food parcels for very needy old folk in South West London.

The campaign for a licence stepped up a gear in an unexpected way. It was because of an 11 year old boy called Sammy Wheeler.

Sammy was a delightful lad who suffered from Muscular Dystrophy and had been confined to a wheelchair for four years. His condition was slowly and inexorably deteriorating and there was little that his parents, or his doctors could do for him.

This didn't detract from the fact that he was a highly intelligent young boy who had an abiding passion for space rockets and in particular the U.S. Space Shuttle.

PICTURED above, comedian Ken Dodd presents a cheque for £2,500 to the Royal Marsden Hospital, Fulham, from Radio Jackie.

The money, towards a scanner appeal, was raised in three months during a live "on-air" auction for two hours each Saturday.

In the picture, left to right: Tracey Moore, Stuart Jeffries, Ken Dodd, Lady Diana Loram and Sir David Loram.

Ken Dodd presents a cheque to the Royal Marsden Hospital

One of the ambitions of Sammy was to see a space shuttle launched. However, they were launched in Florida and the cost of going there was prohibitive. There was no way that his parents could find the money to fulfil his dream. The situation was heartbreaking.

Tony met with his parents and, after a long discussion with Dave Owen, worked out the basis of an appeal to raise the necessary cash.

The first problem was going to be finding suitable accommodation near the space shuttle launch site.

Tony contacted John Bonny of the Leatherhead Lions Club who made some urgent trans-Atlantic phone calls and arranged for the Wheelers to stay with an American family for free. Then it was simply the challenge of raising the £1,000 needed to buy the tickets. We set about this task with purpose. The clock was ticking. NASA was not going to delay the launch for us. The money started to come in.

The campaign hit the television screens within days.

The 6 o'clock Show with Michael Aspel and Janet Street-Porter, interviewed Jackie supporters, Penny Ashton and Stuart Jefferies. They told Michael Aspel that they were doing a sponsored slim for the Radio Jackie Sammy Wheeler Appeal. This was emphasised by the fact that Penny and Stuart were wearing Radio Jackie tee shirts. Michael Aspel talked about the appeal and referred in the warmest tones to Radio Jackie.

The appeal was successful and soon Sammy was waiting at Heathrow Airport for the flight to Florida. The television cameras were all there.

Sammy Wheeler

Robin Houston for Thames Television News reported that Sammy was going to have a ringside seat for the space shuttle launch, courtesy of Radio Jackie.

Andrew Gardner for IRN reported that Radio Jackie had raised the £1,000.

Meanwhile, the BBC, snooty as ever, covered the story in detail but simply said that the money was raised by 'Friends and Family'! No mention of Radio Jackie.

The trip to Florida was a resounding success. The Wheeler family arrived back at Heathrow Airport, tired but with broad smiles all over their faces. Sammy, in particular was thrilled and repeated that he had always wanted to see the space shuttle launched. He described the launch as 'noisy'.

Andrew Gardner reports the Sammy Wheeler story for Thames Television

Now Radio Jackie had stuck its head above the parapet. All the London commercial television stations were comfortably talking about us and soon the politicians began to rally to our cause.

Maggie Nelson for London Plus News reported that the Liberals and the Tories on the Kingston Council had overwhelmingly voted to support Radio Jackie's bid for a licence.

Council Spokesman, Roger Hayes (Liberal) said, *'From our point of view, the reason that we would support an illegal act of this sort is because we don't believe the law is right in this area.'*

This simple statement said it all. Coming from the Kingston Council was all the more telling. They were prepared to endorse our illegal act of broadcasting because they all believed that the law was wrong.

Later in the interview, Roger Hayes was asked whether Radio Jackie was simply a parasite? He paused for a moment before giving his considered reply, which was, *'Parasites means they are feeding off the living.'* He paused, then, *'No. I think they provide a necessary service locally and we would much prefer to see that done on a legal basis so that they can run a useful service for the local community; a service that the local community can be involved with.'*

We gained the support of most of the local, district, and county counsellors. Local MPs gave us their support, most noticeably Angela Rumbold, who was highly regarded in the Margaret Thatcher administration and was a cabinet minister. She recorded several appeals for Radio Jackie to be given a licence and these were subsequently broadcast. We obtained 50,000 signatures on this petition.

**M.P. for Merton, Angela Rumbold, talks to Tony Collis
outside the Radio Jackie shop**

Angela Rumbold was one of the Thatcherite breed of right-of-centre, 'free enterprise' politicians. Her own personal views were very much in line with the thinking of the government of the day.

She met frequently with Tony Collis and they had established a natural rapport.

Through her, we had the ear of the Minister responsible for broadcasting, Norman Tebbitt (The Chingford Skinhead) of the Department of Trade and Industry (D.T.I.)

Norman Tebbitt was obviously not going to take any further action against Radio Jackie. He viewed it as an interesting experiment in local commercial radio that had a 'free enterprise' aspect that he heartily applauded. For the moment Jackie was safe but we were still no nearer to getting a licence.

Radio stations use a market research organisation called RAJAR in order to determine the size of their audience. These figures are released quarterly and, depending upon the actual numbers of people listening, advertising rates are set accordingly. The more listeners, the higher the rate for advertising goes.

In those years, there were four music stations in the Jackie area. BBC Radios One and Two, Capital Radio in London and Radio Mercury in Crawley.

Poll supports Radio Jackie

BANNED broadcasters Radio Jackie have been given and overwhelming vote of support from Sutton residents.

A High Street survey carried out by Conservative councillor for Cheam West, Ken Cole, revealed that eight out of ten people had listened to the pirate station, with 75 per cent of those tuning-in regularly.

The survey also showed that suppport for Radio Jackie was maintained across all ranges, with 129 people's opinions canvassed, from young teenagers to the elderly.

Interestingly, over 16 per cent of the interviewees said that the attitude of political candidates towards the outlawed station would affect the

by Neil Roberts

way they voted in a local election.

The station, which celebrated its 16th birthday on Tuesday (19), is continuing the campaign for a licence to broadcast to South West London.

In a detailed 18-page booklet entitled "Encouraging Growth and Competition in the UK Radio Industry," the station has set out the thinking and background behind its application.

Banstead and Sutton News
6th February 1985

It was apparent that all four stations had lost audience and that this had gone across to Radio Jackie. A conservative guess estimated the audience for Jackie at around 30% or a quarter of a million listeners. This was rivalling the listening figures of the all powerful Radio Two.

The apocryphal story that emerged at the time was that the Chairmen of Capital Radio and John Aumonier, Managing Director of Radio Mercury, sought a meeting with Norman Tebbitt.

'Mr Tebbitt,' they protested, 'this Radio Jackie is stealing all our listeners!'

Norman Tebbitt is reputed to have replied, 'If they are stealing all your listeners then I suspect that I have given the licence to the wrong people. I suggest you get out there and compete.'

Quite whether this happened or not is unclear but the response is entirely consistent with the 'on your bike' philosophy of Norman Tebbitt.

However, what is certain, is that John Aumonier stated on Thames Weekend News that Radio Jackie had grown to a serious proportion and was 'sophisticated and dangerous in their commercial activities.'

It was concluded that the main 'beef' was with the D.T.I. and that getting appropriate legal action was a long drawn out affair.

It was even reported that Margaret Thatcher had suggested to Lord Thompson, the Chairman of the IBA, that Radio Jackie should be given a licence. Lord Thompson pre-empted this by issuing the following statement:-

'... (Stations like Radio Jackie) ... *are illegal predators who steal news bulletins, pay no copyright fees, avoid nationally agreed union rates of pay, and ignore advertising standards.*'

He was not going to back down from that position.

Given the right to reply by the Channel 4 Diverse Reports, 'This Week' programme, Tony Collis said, "*Really, I think the IBA stations are over-financed and over-engineered and are too lavish. Small businesses cannot afford to set up small stations ... (as a result) ... half of ILR stations are foreign owned. Radio Jackie does its best to operate within the law. We pay PAYE and VAT. We just need a licence set at a level that the listeners can support.*'

He then added, '*I have offered to pay IRN...(for their news)... but they refused.*'

104

The IBA, determined to get the last words, then issued the following statement:-

'...*land-based pirate stations were free to bid for independent local radio franchises, but preferred to open illegally and avoid paying the costs of legal radio stations.*'

Nick Higham, Radio Editor of Broadcast Magazine, when asked, '*As in the 60s, pirate radio led to changes in established radio, the same could be happening now?*' replied, '*It looks like it – YES.*'

Radio Jackie was going from strength to strength. The listening base was huge. The support was passionate. Almost one in every four cars was displaying a Radio Jackie car sticker. The signal was strong. The politicians were behind us. Cabinet Ministers were behind us. Even Norman Tebbitt was on our side.

Surely it was just a matter of time before we got our licence.

And then the IRA exploded the Brighton bomb at the Conservative Party Conference.

CHAPTER THIRTY-FOUR

Norman Tebbitt and his wife were seriously injured in the explosion and soon there was a statement made that he would withdraw from frontline politics. Our support at the 'top table' had gone.

Leon Britten was appointed as Norman Tebbitt's replacement. He was a QC and a very different 'kettle of fish'.

The dark clouds were gathering.

The political idealism of Norman Tebbitt had gone and in its place was a man who, by his training and profession, instinctively had a regard for the law and maintaining the rule of law.

Our days were numbered.

The 50,000 signature petition was handed in to Leon Britten. Politicians lobbied. The listeners followed our situation with increasing passion and interest.

Radio Jackie had struck a chord with the population of South West London and North Surrey and they were determined that we should stay.

It wasn't long before the Wireless Telegraphy Act was amended to outlaw our activities.

But still nothing happened. A month passed and we were still on the air. Were we going to be made an exception? Were we going to be given a licence that would exclude us from the terms of this new Act of Parliament? We didn't know.

There was a change of tack. Tony Collis received a 'tip-off' that the situation had become a great deal more serious. The informant told him that there was an injunction about to be served requiring him to cease ownership of an illegal radio station.

The Home Office had decided to go for the owner, via the courts, rather than risk a high profile raid on an extremely popular pirate.

It was obvious that the injunction could be served at any moment and if it was served then he would have to close Radio Jackie down straight away or risk severe penalties.

Tony called all of us together, well away from the studios, and outlined the situation. It was grim.

'The positive side of this is that they are going for me and not the station.' Tony declared. 'Therefore we can stay on the air until they catch up with me and serve the injunction.'

Dave Owen turned to Tony; he knew what this meant. 'You have to go into hiding, Tony.'

Tony smiled. 'I am in hiding, as of now.'

'Right!'

'I can't go home.'

'You shouldn't even drive your car. If you get stopped in that...'

'Hmm... This is going to be tough.'

'You can sleep at my place tonight but tomorrow you must move on. I'll be the first place they will look once they realise that you're not going home.'

Later that afternoon, a car drew up outside the studio. Two men got out and asked for Tony Collis. Of course, they were told he was not there. The car parked outside his house all that night. By 10 a.m., it had gone.

It was around this time that Tony was climbing over the back fence of Dave Owen's garden and into a waiting car. He was whisked away to a safer house.

The two men returned to the studio later in the day. This was a determined attempt to serve the injunction.

The following six weeks saw Tony moving from house to house, being spirited away in the back of cars and vans.

On one occasion, they knocked on the front door as Tony was climbing over the back wall. He had nowhere to go so he strolled into a nearby pub, ordered a pint and made a phone call to arrange the next move.

Communications were complicated. A simple phone call might have led the authorities to where he was hiding out. However, Radio Jackie was still on the air and needed his leadership and direction. This soon settled down into calls from phone boxes to known sympathisers who then passed on the messages.

A fast getaway

Six weeks is a long time to be in hiding. There were many things that needed to be handled but Tony was unable to do this because of the situation. Everyday things like clean clothes and having a shower were however not a problem. There were more than a hundred people who willingly helped. No doubt there were thousands more, had they been asked.

All the time Radio Jackie stayed on the air, but it was becoming clear to staff and listeners alike that the situation could not continue for much longer.

The last throw of the dice was going to have to be passing the ownership of the station to somebody else. The question was, who?

Dave Cliff finally resolved the problem by suggesting to Tony that my brother Robin (Phil Hazelton), who lived in Holland was the best person to purchase the station. He was perfect because he was outside the jurisdiction of English law, yet committed to the Jackie cause.

Tony organised a meeting with his solicitor and instructed him to draw up a 'Bill of Sale' for Radio Jackie. He duly obliged and Tony set off into the night, clutching the document, for a clandestine meeting at midnight in Bexhill.

Tony did not tell anyone what he was planning. In fact, at risk of being stopped, he drove to Bexhill in his own car and met Robin who had driven over from Holland.

Robin handed over a cheque and together they signed the 'Bill of Sale'. Tony was no longer the owner of Radio Jackie. Robin climbed back into his car and caught the 4 a.m. ferry from Dover. Radio Jackie Ltd was now a Dutch-owned company.

Tony, tired and relieved, returned to his home for the first time in six weeks. He opened the front door, climbed the stairs and fell into his own bed. He slept through well into the afternoon.

When Tony walked into the studio, we all looked up with shock. We knew that something was up but he calmly told us to carry on as normal, which we did.

Radio Jackie was still on the air.

It was not until the following day that the authorities finally caught up with Tony and served the injunction. Tony protested but the deed was done.

Once again he calmly said, 'Carry on as normal.'

Radio Jackie was still on the air.

Five days later, Tony received a summons requiring him to attend court to explain why he had not complied with the terms of the injunction.

He attended the court where he explained that he was not the owner of the station, at the time that the injunction had been served, and therefore he was not in a position to close it down.

He produced the 'Bill of Sale' and a bank statement showing the transfer of money. There were exasperated glances around the court when it was revealed that the new owner was resident outside the UK.

All parties withdrew to consider their positions.

Radio Jackie was still on the air.

Nothing happened immediately. However, after about six weeks, we received a 'tip-off' that we were going to be raided.

It duly came.

The Home Office officials arrived accompanied by a large number of police wearing body armour and 'tooled-up' for a fight. They had been told that they were not sure what to expect. THEY COULD BE TERRORISTS.

They stormed into Abbotts Road, Dave Owen's mother's house.

Dave greeted them, 'Hello, I've been expecting you.'

A policeman pounced on him, flung him to the floor and sat on him to prevent him from moving.

'Don't you dare move or you're "dead meat"!'

Initially winded, Dave soon caught his breath and looked at him. 'Isn't this a bit over the top? I mean, you know that all you are doing is closing down Radio Jackie?'

The policeman leapt up in surprise. 'Radio Jackie? I won a tee-shirt on your station last week – does this mean I'm not going to get it?'

Radio Jackie is raided

Department of Trade and Industry investigators raided Radio Jackie, one of the most successful land-based pirate stations at midday yesterday, confiscated more than £10,000-worth of equipment and putting the station off the air.

Nine people were interviewed and warned that they could face prosecution. Mr Peter Rivers, for the station, based at Cheam, south London, said it would be broadcasting today.

Pirate Jackie stormed by raiders

By ALEX HENDRY,

A PIRATE radio station was swept off the air yesterday by a Government raiding party.

Radio Jackie DJ Ron Brown was playing a record when the station's front door came off its hinges.

He broadcast : " I think we have visitors." Then Radio Jackie was off the air—again. The station broadcasts in South West London and claims 200,000 listeners every week. Since 1972 there have been 24 prosecutions against it.

Last night station co-ordinator Peter Rivers said : " We want to get back in business as soon as possible."

Listener Ian Courdery, of Kingston Road, Tolworth, Surrey, said : " I was at the station to take part in a quiz. Suddenly there was a lot of banging and a secretary rushed into the studio and yelled : ' We're being raided '."

The offices and studio are above a travel agents in the High Street, Worcester Park, Surrey.

Raid puts `pirates' off the air

A POLICE raid pulled the plug yesterday on Radio Jackie — Britain's longest - running pirate station.

The London-based station's transmitter and record collection were seized from studios in Worcester Park.

And last night police were quizzing nine people who may face prosecution.

Radio Jackie, which claimed to have 250,000 listeners in South West London, had been running for 15 years.

Radio pirate sunk after police raid

by Adrian Shaw

RADIO JACKIE, London's longest - running illegal radio station, was closed down in a raid by the Department of Trade and Industry today.

Thousands of pounds' worth of broadcasting equipment was seized. Staff were warned that they may be prosecuted under the 1949 Wireless Telegraphy Act.

Radio Jackie, which has led a campaign for a relaxation of the laws covering local radio, went off the air at 11.27 a.m.

The station's bosses said they hoped to be broadcasting again soon. Radio Jackie had been broadcasting to South-west London from offices in Central Road, Worcester Park, round the clock, for seven days a week.

Some of the many reports that appeared in the national dailies, *Times*, *Express*, *Telegraph* and *Sun*

CHAPTER THIRTY-FIVE

We replaced the transmitter and carried on.

The next raid came the following day. This time they stormed the studio in Worcester Park, as well as the transmitter site. They confiscated all the studio equipment, also the transmitter.

Things were getting serious.

Tony had been talking to Angela Rumbold and other contacts within the government. It was clear that this was the end. However, he was assured that if he made another application for a licence it would be favourably received. It was presented to him that it might be a 'shutdown' for a few weeks whilst a licence was sorted out.

That evening Tony gathered everyone to a meeting. We agreed that the time had come to cease broadcasting. We also agreed that we needed formally to apply for a licence, once again.

We also agreed that we needed to put out one final, farewell broadcast, which we did.

We made it abundantly clear that we were going to be closed down and that this was 'Goodbye'. Crowds immediately began to gather at the studios. Everyone knew where we were so the support was immediate and substantial. Hundreds of listeners gathered to watch and try to bar the way of the Home Office and police to the studio.

We decided that the closedown was going to be at 7 p.m. We began saying our farewells. There were tears and chants of support from the street outside. We made it perfectly clear that we were going to close the station finally at that time and that we were not going to start again until we had a licence.

The Home Office arrived, accompanied by the police, at about 6.30 p.m., half an hour before the 'Closedown'. The crowd was huge. Police estimates put it at 500 people, many eye-witnesses suggest it was nearer a thousand. The reality was that Central Road in Worcester Park was blocked by the throng.

There were prolonged discussions between the Home Office and the police. We watched from the window. They were not sure what to do. If ever 'People Power' succeeded, then this was it. The Police flatly

Radio Jackie back on air

A PIRATE radio station went back on the air yesterday despite an attempt by Department of Trade and Industry investigators to close it down. Less than 24 hours after £10,000 worth of equipment was seized in a raid by five men from the Ministry, Radio Jackie in South West London resumed transmission.

Station staff vowed to carry on broadcasting despite the threat of £2,000 fines and three-month prison sentences.

The country's longest running land-based pirate station claims 200,000 listeners and has been broadcasting illegally since 1969 from above travel agents in Worcester Park.

Station co-ordinator Mr Peter Rivers, 25, said : " We will not be intimidated by bully boy tactics. This raid has made us even more determined to keep going."

A Department of Trade and Industry spokesman said : " Legislation passed last year impowers us to carry out the kind of action we have taken against Radio Jackie. The station is broadcasting illegally and the law must be seen to prevail. If this station is broadcasting again we will take similar action."

Sunday Express
3rd February, 1985

111

refused to let the Home Office officials make a move on the grounds of not being able to maintain public order.

The mood that the crowd was in would have surely meant a riot if they had made a single move in our direction. They would have been torn limb from limb. It was a stalemate.

However, the Home Office and the Police had a separate team raiding the transmitter site in Abbotts Road.

So, in spite of announcing that the station would close at 7 o'clock, the Home Office raided with only a few minutes to go.

There was a hurried phone call to the studio telling us about the raid and that the transmitter could go off the air at any moment.

Tears flow as Radio Jackie goes off air

RADIO Jackie, whose premises have been raided three times since Friday by Department of Trade and Industry officials, finally went off the air on Monday evening and told its listeners it would not be back without a licence.

It was an emotional finale with staff and listeners in tears at the studio and offices in Central Road, Worcester Park.

The founder of Radio Jackie, Mr. Tony Collis, said it was the fore-runner of small radio stations proving that millions of pounds were not required to broadcast.

It has raised tens of thousands of pounds for charity and involved listeners as much

as possible, he said. "They don't have any other local station they can relate to."

Mr. Collis has been encouraged by the support given to the radio by local people, who have telephoned and demonstrated at the studio since the raids.

In particular Mr. Collis considered the final raid by the Radio Investigation Service to be totally unnecessary. For it was made in spite of the radio's public declaration that it was closing down voluntarily that evening and would apply for a licence.

Mr. Collis was surprised by the tactics of the officials, who have smashed down doors to break in. "They are not dealing with terrorists and drug offenders but people who help the local community to a very great extent," he said.

Eighteen members of staff at the pirate radio station now face the dole.

Midweek Comet
6th February, 1985

The studio was packed with the public and staff, so too were the stairs. The crowd was chanting; cheering our every word and booing the Police and Home Office.

Dave Owen was the final voice on the station. He spoke of the raid that was happening at the transmitter site and that we could go off the air at any moment. Dave just managed to get out, 'I suppose, this is goodbye, I hope we meet again real soon.'

Click

Silence

Nothing.

Geoff Rogers, one of our presenters, cycled round to the Abbotts Road site nearly an hour later. There was a Police car parked in a nearby side road and in the back sat the unmistakeable figure of Eric Gotts.

SCHEMES outside Radio Jackie's station on Friday when officials from the Department of Trade and Industry backed by police raided the premises silencing the airway pirates. Pictures by John Stuart.

SWITCHED OFF!

Radio pirates are silenced after raid

THE PLUG was pulled on Radio Jackie last Friday when officials from the Department of Trade and Industry raided the pirate station.

A defiant attempt by the staff to continue broadcasting was quashed on Sunday when officials raided the premises again.

Radio Jackie, which has been illegally broadcasting on 227m/1323 khz since 1969, suddenly went dead at 11 am last Friday. Puzzled listeners trying to phone in were unable to get any replies except occasionally a curt request to hang up.

Five men from the Ministry moved in with two policemen and seized more than £10,000 worth of equipment.

Less than 24 hours later the pirate station was back on the air and station co-ordinator Peter Rivers, 25, was declaring: "We will not be intimidated by bully boy tactics. This raid has made us even more determined to keep going."

The Department of Trade and Industry retaliated by again raiding the premises above an estate agents in Central Road, Worcester Park.

A spokesman for the Ministry said: "Legislation passed last year impowers us to carry out the kind of action we have taken against Radio Jackie. The station is broadcasting illegally and the law must be seen to prevail."

Nine people now face prosecution and the threat of up to £2,000 fines and three-month prison sentences.

Radio Jackie is the longest running land-based pirate station and claims to have 200,000 listeners. It has recently been campaigning for a licence to broadcast to south-west London.

CHAPTER THIRTY-SIX

Tony had registered Radio Jackie Limited as a company. He had carefully maintained accounts, which we had submitted each year. We were registered for VAT and PAYE. We made all payments on time and for the correct amounts. We had even made payments to the Performing Rights Society but they refused to accept the cheques.

In fact, we had run the whole operation as a proper legal business: a legal radio station. The only law we broke was the Wireless Telegraphy Act and that was the law that needed changing.

That night we desperately needed a cup of Molly Catford's tea. She didn't let us down.

We were shattered. The dream, that so nearly came true, had been

Putney Series, Thursday February 7, 1985 Page 4

Guardian Graphics House, Adela Avenue, Motspur Park.

Jackie killed for doing too well

SO they have finally done it, after 16 years Radio Jackie has been closed down.

But the officials from the Department of Trade who kicked in the doors of Jackie were not acting on their own initiative.

Somewhere on high, the word got round, Jackie is a local radio station which is doing just too well.

Jackie does not pay huge sums of money to the Independent Broadcasting Authority for the privilege of entertaining South West London.

Jackie is taking money away from the "approved" — and licensed stations.

Over the next weeks we can expect more raids on "pirate" stations.

If the Department of Trade and others gets their way we will once again have the "choice" of radio stations who wouldn't recognise Tooting High Street if it jumped up and tap danced on their turntables.

London is a vast city, the concerns of people in Balham are very different to those in Barking or Hampstead.

Just as we are a local newspaper serving a need in this area, so Jackie was a local radio station.

It served a need and that need does not disappear after the Department of Trade's clampdown.

The Guardian,
8th February 1985

cruelly snatched away from us. We were now further back than we had been all those years before, when Dave, Mike Hayes and Nick Catford had wheeled the pram around Morden Hall Park. At least, if we had been raided then, there was the reality of another broadcast the following Sunday.

The Jackie studio after the raid

Now it was all over. We were in our thirties, we were no longer those lads that we used to be. Somehow the thought of running Radio Jackie as a Sunday pirate was not an option. We had grown up.

Molly beamed, 'Now come on boys, let's all have a nice cuppa tea.' We all trooped into 77 Burleigh Road and her tea never tasted so good.

'Now what we have to do, boys, is to decide what we are going to do next. We have come this far. We mustn't stop now.' She looked around the room. We nodded but we all had a bitter taste in our mouths and it had nothing to do with Molly's tea.

Really, it was over to Tony and how well he could mobilise the political forces of South West London behind a campaign to get us licenced. If it was to succeed, it was going to have to happen quickly or else Radio Jackie would be forgotten.

Tony worked tirelessly towards putting in an impressive bid for a licence.

Pirate's bid to get legal air

By KERRY ANSELL

THE Worcester Park based pirate station Radio Jackie, is being forced to play the waiting game in its bid to go legal.

They will not hear until December whether their bid for a licence has been successful.

Five licences are to be granted for community radio stations throughout London and Radio Jackie are optimistic about their chances of winning one.

"We hope that we have established that there is a demand in the area and that we are able to run a sensible radio service," said station co-ordinator Peter Stremes.

They have put in a formal licence application in the shape of a 40-page report.

Radio Jackie has been off the air since February when the station was closed down following a series of raids by Department of Trade Officials.

It was founded in 1969 and has always campaigned to be made legal.

Before its shut-down the station was broadcasting around the clock.

Wallington and Sutton Advertiser

The formal bid went in. It was a beautifully prepared document, well presented. It discussed all the aspects of running a local commercial station and drew upon the immense experience that we had gained over the previous few years.

Surely this had to succeed.

But, NO.

After endless discussions, in which Angela Rumbold and many of the leading local counsellors rallied to our cause, the government decided to shelve the issue. Small local commercial stations were simply not on the Radio Authority's agenda at that time.

Tony continued with his fruit machine business. It proved highly lucrative. He also found time to install the transmitters on the Radio Caroline boat, *Ross Revenge*.

The rest of us went our separate ways although we stayed very much in touch with each other.

Tony Collis when he was transmitter engineer for Radio Caroline

I was married with three children at this point and had moved into the computer industry selling IBM mainframe computers and later large mini-computers for Mc-Donnell Douglas.

Radio Jackie was just a failed dream.

In 1997 the Radio Authority advertised a licence for the Kingston area of South West London and North Surrey and we just knew that our time had come. This was 'our licence'.

Tony put together another extremely well thought through licence application. Again there was a series of endless discussions.

Things went quiet, whilst the decision was made. We 'knew' this was going to be our licence.

Tony started to get the team together ready for the re-launch of Radio Jackie.

AN APPLICATION TO THE HOME SECRETARY FOR AN EXPERIMENTAL LICENCE TO OPERATE A LOCAL RADIO SERVICE FOR SOUTH-WEST LONDON

Presented by

The front cover of Radio Jackie's formal application for a licence

Then came another bitter blow. The decision was made by the Radio Authority to hand the licence to Radio Investments in the name of Thames FM.

We were resigned at this stage to never getting our licence. It seemed that the last chance had eluded us and that we were doomed to fail.

Thames FM duly came on the air. It was very bland and nothing like the bright music radio station that Radio Jackie had been and wanted to be again.

Then, at the end of 2002, word leaked out that Thames FM was in financial trouble and that Radio Investments were looking to sell it. Certainly it was losing listeners because the RAJAR figures revealed the audience to be at 7,000. That is almost within a sampling error of being NIL.

Tony Collis contacted as many of his influential business and political friends as possible to try to put together a bid. As before, he insisted on owning the station totally. His was the risk.

Gradually the 'asking price' for Thames FM was whittled down until eventually Tony agreed to buy the station for £1 but accepted all the on-going liabilities, such as wages, rent and the Performing Rights Society.

The Radio Authority was extremely concerned about the station sound and its speech content. Tony was adamant. Radio Jackie was a 'music radio' station and had to be free to broadcast without any restrictions imposed upon it. He pointed out that Thames FM had failed and that the whole future of local commercial radio now hung on the success of small independent stations like Radio Jackie. We had to be free to broadcast what we wanted, restricted only by a commitment to serve the local people and to be providing a local news service.

The Radio Authority was uneasy but eventually they nodded.

I received a phone call that evening from Tony, 'I am now going to have to set up a serious advertising sales team, can you help me?'

CAN YOU HELP ME? HUH! My whole life had been waiting for this moment and it was amazing just how convenient it was with my work commitments. I was an independent IT consultant by then and I was coming to the end of a six-month contract. All I had to do was to tell the company that I did not intend to renew.

So within a couple of weeks, I was a full time employee of Radio Jackie

Radio Jackie had got its licence.

CHAPTER THIRTY-SEVEN

I gazed around the offices and the studios. It was just what Tony and I had dreamed about all those years before.

It was on the high street, in this case Tolworth Broadway. Tony had sensibly purchased outright the freehold of the derelict Post Office. If everything else failed, at least he would have the property: a sensible businessman.

Six months of intensive work had elapsed. The first things to be transferred to this new building were the studios. They were built within a few days and were operational within a week. This meant that Tony could divest himself of the expensive property that had housed Thames FM.

After that it was a matter of sustaining the station whilst working in a building site.

We retained the name of Thames FM for those few months, whilst Dave Owen, who was once again the Programme Controller, worked ceaselessly to prepare the new sound of Radio Jackie. Music needed to be put on computer, jingles and station imaging needed to be prepared for the launch.

Gone were the days of vinyl discs. CDs were also really a thing of the past. They were on the shelf for emergencies. Today's radio is on computer. But Dave Owen's Radio Jackie was special. He tightened up all the music links on the computer, so that the station would sound more purposeful and dynamic.

This was going to be REAL music radio.

Today was the day that we launched Radio Jackie as a legal entity, fully licenced.

I looked around the office, it was gradually filling up with all the old faces from the past. Brian Horne was joking as usual. Dave Cliff was smiling yet quiet with emotion. Kevin Stewart was flitting back and forth with a glass in his hand. There were so many familiar faces: Steve Mowbray, Roger Mowbray's son, Kelvin Michaels, Mike Hayes and, of course, the man who had started it all in the first place, Nick Catford.

There was still a little time to go before we came back on air again as Radio Jackie.

Nick Catford

I looked at Tony and together we lifted the six-foot-high model pirate out of the front door and onto the pavement of Tolworth Broadway. We had both agreed that when Radio Jackie had its licence, we would have this pirate outside the door to remind us of our roots. We felt that, as long as the pirate was there, we would not forget how hard we had struggled to get this licence.

The office was buzzing. It was a huge open-plan office with a large 107.8 Radio Jackie mural on the wall.

Just inside the front door was the main studio. Beautifully laid out with touch screens, Sky Television, telephone switchboard for the studio, a computer for collecting emails and three microphones. The second studio was behind the main one and was a mirror image. This was used for news readers and simple production work. Complex production work was done by Dave Owen at his studio in the same shed in Abbotts Road that had housed the transmitters all those years before.

The clock was ticking. It was approaching 12 noon. We had not mentioned the name of Thames FM for some days now as we counted down to the re-launch.

Five minutes to midday and gradually we began winding down the old station.

With just thirty seconds to go, we went off the air.

Silence

Then at precisely 12 o'clock, we played 'Love Theme', the same piece of music that we had started with back in 1969. It was a hugely emotional moment.

Everyone looked a little wet in the eyes and were puffing hard to stem the tears.

I looked across towards the desks outside the studio.

Sitting there was Molly Catford and her husband Jack. Jack was well into his nineties by now and Molly was fast catching him up. They had seen it all and now they had survived to witness Radio Jackie as a licenced station.

I don't mind admitting that I still shed a tear of emotion at the thought of that moment.

Those cups of tea, the moments when she had, quite literally, persuaded us to carry on the fight, the unswerving support of her 'boys', her total faith in us and what we were doing, her boundless optimism.

**Jack and Molly Catford at the 2003 launch.
Colin King is in the centre.**

A couple of the guys suggested that we needed to post lookouts and we all laughed.

We had made it.

Dave Owen, who was the last voice on Radio Jackie when we were closed before, was the natural choice to re-open the station.

He lifted the fader, '...now as I was saying before I was so rudely interrupted...'

'Across South West London and North Surrey, live from Tolworth Tower, this is 107.8 Radio Jackie.'

Tony Collis celebrating

CHAPTER THIRTY-EIGHT

THE EPILOGUE

The return of Radio Jackie was BIG news in South West London.

It was on the front page of every local paper, together with photographs, both past and present. There was also extensive coverage inside.

Radio Jackie had always wanted to be a local radio station supporting local people and local businesses.

I was therefore determined to wave the Radio Jackie 'flag' wherever I could.

It was a very emotional time, attending Business Breakfasts for the local Chambers of Commerce, Kingston, Richmond, Wandsworth and Surrey.

I genuinely did not know what my reception would be like amongst the business community. At these breakfast meetings you are allowed to stand up and talk about your business for 60 seconds only.
I nervously rose to my feet and asked whether anybody had heard of Radio Jackie?

The response was amazing; they clapped and cheered. They were so supportive that even now I feel a tear of emotion, just recalling it.

There are some phenomenal people in our area. There are some brilliant and innovative businesses.

There are also amazing characters. For instance, the UK Super Street Bike Champion of 2003 operating from the back of a little hardware store in Alexander Drive, Berrylands.

The Secombe Theatre was on its knees and really struggling to survive. Coming from the 'Goon' generation, it bothered me that the great man (who had supported Radio Jackie) Harry Secombe's memorial should be failing in this way.

With our help it is on the way up again. I am so happy.

But Radio Jackie has always been a little local radio station, run by local people for local people. It is still quirky but it is still fiercely independent. It is still run by Tony Collis who is at the same time both inspirational and exasperating.

But what the heck? We made it.

AND FINALLY

About three months after the re-launch, there was a bustle of activity.

'Tidy up guys.'

We ran the vacuum cleaner over the floor and arranged papers into neat piles. Brian Angus, the Mayor of Epsom and Ewell was about to make a formal visit to the station.

We carried on with our work ... work that is endless, 24 hours per day, 7 days per week. Programmes, News, Advertising, it never stops. Radio is a never-ending conveyor belt.

The mayor's car drew up outside and Brian Angus emerged wearing his best suit and his impressive chains of office. With him were two officials from the council.

'Good morning, I'm Brian Angus, I'm here to see Tony Collis.'

I found Tony and introduced them. They sat down and began chatting.

Boys and their toys!

Within five minutes, the two of them were flying Tony's model airship: a remote controlled blimp. Lighter than air, they steered it around the office, bumping into various members of staff, to chortles of laughter.

Soon they got tired of flying that and Tony produced his remote-controlled flying saucer.

Steered by a gun-like handset, they were able to direct it around the office.

ZZZzzzzzzooommmm. Up it went. Down it went. Along it went.

Suddenly there was a wail from Tony. 'Where's the blimp?'
We all looked around. It was nowhere to be seen.

'We left it by the wall over there.' He pointed to the wall with the mural.

We searched everywhere. The blimp had vanished.

'It must have got caught in an air current and drifted out of the front door.'

Tony and the Mayor rushed to the front door and looked out.

There, about twenty feet above the ground and tangled in the branches of the tree outside, was the blimp. Tony tried to climb the tree but in vain.

Then he spied a climbing frame being used by some decorators who were working on a shop some five or six doors away.

They happily agreed for us to borrow it, so Tony and the Mayor pushed it down to the tree.
Tony immediately climbed to the top and then attempted to clamber onto the branch holding the blimp.

I rushed indoors and picked up a long pole with a hook on the end, used for opening windows, and handed it to the Mayor, who was, by now, halfway up the climbing frame.

He then passed it to Tony who stretched out with it to reach the blimp.

So there was Tony, once again up a tree. There was the Mayor of Epsom & Ewell, in his best suit and wearing his chain of office, half way up the climbing frame, saying, 'Up a bit Tony. No, along a bit - you're nearly there, Tony. No up a bit... no down a bit!'

The End.

ADDENDUM

THE FUN GOES ON...

This edition was reprinted in 2017 and against all the odds, after 14 years, Radio Jackie still flourishes. It has a licence that secures its future well into the next decade.

Tony Collis

ABOUT THE AUTHOR

Colin King was born in Bromley in Kent during the bitterly cold winter of 1947. In 1957, his family moved to Norfolk where he attended the King Edward VI School in Norwich.

Shortly after leaving school he moved to Brockham in North Surrey where he discovered the two passions of his life: radio and cricket.

Angered by the banning of the offshore pirates, Colin joined the Free Radio Association and served on the Committee. He hosted the rallies in Trafalgar Square in 1968, 1969 and 1970. He also was a junior member of the team that made representations to the Heath Government's Green Paper Committee on the future of broadcasting within the UK.

He went on to found the ground-breaking land-based pirate station, Radio Kaleidoscope and, of course, worked with Radio Jackie.

Radio took him back to Norfolk when he was appointed Station Manager of North Norfolk Radio.

More recently he returned to Radio Jackie to help re-launch the station in 2003. He could be heard on most weekday evenings reading the news. He has since retired.

Colin has an abiding love of village cricket. In 1999 he was elected chairman of the Mid-Norfolk Sunday Cricket League, a small rural league that had only seven member clubs. The League has flourished since then and now boasts ten divisions and 80 clubs.

Colin married the love of his life, Angie, in 1977 and they have three children, Grant, Anne-Marie and Sylvie. They also have seven grandchildren: Jake, Ben, James, Amy, Poppy, Sophie and Robert.

1984   **STUDIOS**   **2003**

On a cold February evening in 1985, over a thousand
people stood outside Radio Jackie's offices in
Worcester Park in defiance of the authorities who were
trying to close down the station.

Why were so many people so passionate about, what
was after all, a pirate radio station?

This is the amazing story of Radio Jackie and its 34 year
battle to bring local radio to the people of South West
London and North Surrey.

A "David and Goliath" story that is inspiring as well as
being uniquely English.
It could only have happened in England.

**Published By
The Larks Press
Ordnance Farmhouse
Guist Bottom
Dereham NR20 5PF**

Price £10.00

9 781904 006404